The Shakespeare Gallery: A Reproduction In Commemoration Of The Tercentenary Anniversary Of The Poet's Birth, Mdccclxiv....

John Boydell, Josiah Boydell, Stephen Ayling

Nabu Public Domain Reprints:

You are holding a reproduction of an original work published before 1923 that is in the public domain in the United States of America, and possibly other countries. You may freely copy and distribute this work as no entity (individual or corporate) has a copyright on the body of the work. This book may contain prior copyright references, and library stamps (as most of these works were scanned from library copies). These have been scanned and retained as part of the historical artifact.

This book may have occasional imperfections such as missing or blurred pages, poor pictures, errant marks, etc. that were either part of the original artifact, or were introduced by the scanning process. We believe this work is culturally important, and despite the imperfections, have elected to bring it back into print as part of our continuing commitment to the preservation of printed works worldwide. We appreciate your understanding of the imperfections in the preservation process, and hope you enjoy this valuable book.

THE

SHAKESPEARE

GALLERY.

a

THE STATUE OF SHAKESPEARE.

LOUIS FRANCIS ROUBILIAC.
"INV^T ET SC^T, MDCCLVIII."

This fine work of art was a commission to the Sculptor from Mr. Garrick, and was bequeathed by the actor to the British Museum, in 1778, but not to be removed there until after the death of Mrs. Garrick. Since that event, in 1822, it has formed a part of the art-treasures of the nation, and now stands in the Hall of the building, on the left of the entrance to the Grenville Library.

In J. T. Smith's "Nollekens and His Times," there is an amusing anecdote concerning this statue,—" Mr. Garrick agreed to give Mr. Roubiliac three hundred guineas for it, and the artist was to make use of the best marble he could afford for the money; unfortunately, however, the block turned out full of veins, which rendered the face so hideous to Mr. Garrick, that he declared he could not put it up, as persons might ask, 'What! was Shakespeare marked with mulberries?' Roubiliac assured Mr. Garrick that it was the best marble he could use for the price of the figure; but that, in order to make it agreeable to him, he would cut off the head, and replace it with another, carved from a fine clear piece of marble, which he did, to the great pleasure of his employer."

Allan Cunningham states, "It is said that he (Garrick), in giving instructions to the artist for the statue, put himself into countenance, and then into posture, and desired the astonished sculptor to model away—'for behold,' said he, 'the poet of Avon.'"

There have been only two prints of this statue issued, both from the painting by Adrian Charpentier, wherein it is introduced as an illustrative accessary to a portrait of Roubiliac; the first was engraved by D. Martin, in 1765, the last by W. Holl, in 1827. As far as can be ascertained no other representations whatever, except this recently executed Photograph, are extant. This Photograph, although not a part of the original Shakespeare Gallery, has been introduced here, as an appropriate frontispiece; it has been effected by permission of the Trustees of the Museum, accorded within the last few weeks.

SHAKESPEARE GALLERY:

A REPRODUCTION IN COMMEMORATION OF THE TERCENTENARY ANNIVERSARY OF THE POET'S BIRTH.

MDCCCLXIV.

LONDON:
L. BOOTH, 307 REGENT STREET, W.
AND S. AYLING, 493 OXFORD STREET, W.C.
1864.

LONDON:
STRANGEWAYS AND WALDEN, PRINTERS,
28 Castle St. Leicester Sq.

THE SHAKESPEARE GALLERY:

A REPRODUCTION COMMEMORATIVE OF THE TERCENTENARY ANNIVERSARY,

MDCCCLXIV.

List of Contents.

	PAGES
INTRODUCTION	i–xxxii

PHOTOGRAPHIC ILLUSTRATIONS IN THE INTRODUCTION.

The Frontispiece—Roubiliac's Statue of Shakespeare, now in the British Museum—the Photograph effected by the express permission of the Trustees. It is the only representation of it *alone* extant ...	iv
The Alto-Relievo in front of the Building erected to contain the Pictures, in Pall Mall. Ph. i.	xxii
The Infant Shakespeare attended by Nature and the Passions. Ph. ii.	xxvi
Shakespeare nursed by Tragedy and Comedy. Ph. iii.	xxx

PHOTOGRAPHIC ILLUSTRATIONS OF THE PLAYS.

(EACH ACCOMPANIED BY THE TEXT.)

Comedies.

	PAGES
The Tempest, Phs. I.–IV.	3–15
The Two Gentlemen of Verona, Ph. V.	19
The Merry Wives of Windsor, VI.–X.	23–39
Measure for Measure, XI. XII.	43–47
The Comedy of Errors, XIII.	51
Much Ado about Nothing, XIV.–XVI.	55–63
Love's Labour's Lost, XVII.	67
A Midsummer-Night's Dream, XVIII. XIX.	71–73
The Merchant of Venice, XX. XXI.	79–83
As You Like it, XXII.–XXXII.	86–127
The Taming of the Shrew, XXXIII. XXXIV.	131–135
All's Well that Ends Well, XXXV.	139
Twelfth Night, XXXVI. XXXVII.	143–147
The Winter's Tale, XXXVIII.–XLI.	151–163

Histories.

King John, Ph. XLII.	167
King Richard the Second, Phs. XLIII. XLIV.	171–175
King Henry the Fourth, Part i., XLV.–XLVIII.	179–191
,, ,, ,, Part ii., XLIX.–LI.	195–203
King Henry the Fifth, LII.	207
King Henry the Sixth, Part i., LIII.–LV.	211–219
,, ,, ,, Part ii., LVI. LVII.	223–227
,, ,, ,, Part iii., LVIII.–LXI.	231–243

	PAGES
King Richard the Third, LXI.–LXIV. … … …	247–255
King Henry the Eighth, LXV.–LXVIII. … …	259–271

Tragedies.

Troilus and Cressida, Phs. LXIX. LXX. … …	275–279
Coriolanus, LXXI. LXXII. … … … …	283–287
Titus Andronicus, LXXIII. … … … …	291
Romeo and Juliet, LXXIV.–LXXVI. … …	295–303
Timon of Athens, LXXVII. … … … …	307
Julius Cæsar, LXXVIII. … … … …	311
Macbeth, LXXIX.–LXXXI. … … … …	315–323
Hamlet, LXXXII. LXXXIII. … … …	327–331
King Lear, LXXXIV.–LXXXVI. … … …	335–343
Othello, LXXXVII.–LXXXIX. … … …	347–355
Antony and Cleopatra, XC. XCI. … … …	359–363
Cymbeline, XCII.–XCIV. … … … …	367–373

₊ *The above series of Photographs has been the production of*

Mr. STEPHEN AYLING.

THE SHAKESPEARE GALLERY:

A LIST OF THE ARTISTS ENGAGED IN THE PRODUCTION OF THE ORIGINAL WORK.

※ The Numbers refer to the Photographs, the Originals of which were the productions of the Engravers whose names appear immediately beneath; there are also appended the names of the Painters and Sculptors from whose works those Engravings were made.

Engravers.

Bartolozzi, Francesco, R.A. XXXVII.
Browne, John, XXI.
Burke, Thomas, XCII.
Caldwall, James, LXXII. LXXIX.
Collyer, Joseph, LXVIII.
Earlom, Richard, LXXXIV.
Facius, George Sigmund, and John Gottlieb, XXV. LV. LXXIV. LXXV. XC.
Fittler, James, XL.
Gaugain, Thomas, XCIV.
Hellyer, Thomas, XCI.
Kirk, Thomas, LXXIII.
Legat, Francis, LXIII. LXIX. LXXXIII. LXXXVI.
Leney, William, XXII. XXIX. LX. LXXI. LXXXVIII. LXXXIX.

Michel, John Baptist, LX. LXI.
Middiman, Samuel, XXIII. XXXIX. XLV.
Ogborne, John, XVI. XXV. XXVII. LIV. LIX.
Parker, James, LXXX.
Playter, C. G. XI. XIII. LVI. LVIII.
Ryder, Thomas, IX. XI. XVII. XIX. XXXVI. XLVIII. XLIX. LVIII. LXXXVII.
Ryder, Thomas, jun. XIX.
Scriven, Edward, LXXVIII.
Schiavonetti, Luigi, V. LXX.
Sharp, William, LXXXV.
Simon, John Peter, II. VI. VIII. XVIII. XX. XXVIII. XXX. XXXIV. XXXVIII. XLVII.
Simon, Peter, XII. XIV. XV. XXXII. LXXVI.
Skelton, William, LXIV.
Smith, Benjamin, Intro. i. ii. iii. I. XLIII.
Taylor, Isaac, LXV.
Taylor, Isaac, jun. X.
Thew, Robert, III. VII. XXVI. XXXIII. XLI. XLII. XLIV. XLVI. L. LI. LII. LIII. LV. LVI. LXII. LXVI. LXVII. LXXVII. LXXXI. LXXXII. XCIII.
Tomkins, Peltro William, XXIV.
Watson, Caroline, IV. LVII.
Wilson, W. C. XXXI.

Painters.

Barry, James, R.A. LXXXVI.
Boydell, Josiah, L. LI. LIV. LIX. LXXXIX.
Browne, Mather, XLIII.
Downman, J., R.A. XXII.
Durno, James, IX. XLIX.
Farington, Joseph, XLV.
Fuseli, Henry, R.A. II. XVIII. XIX. LII. LXXIX. LXXXII. LXXXIV.

Graham, James, LXXXVIII.
Hamilton, Gavin, LXXII.
Hamilton, William, R.A. XV. XVII. XXXII. XXXVII. XLI. XCII.
Hodges, William, R.A. XXI. XXIII.
Hoppner, John, R.A. XCIII.
Kauffman, Maria Angelica, R.A. V. LXX.
Kirk, Thomas, XII. LXXIII.
Miller, William, LX. LXXIV.
Northcote, James, R.A. XLII. XLIV. LV. LVIII. LXI. LXII. LXIII. LXIV. LXXVI.
Opie, John, R.A. XXXVIII. LIII. LVI. LXXV. LXXVII.
Peters, the Rev. William, R.A. VII. VIII. XIV. LXVI. LXVIII.
Ramberg, John Henry, XXXVI.
Reynolds, Sir Joshua, President R.A. LVII. LXXXI.
Rigaud, John Francis, R.A. XIII. XLVIII.
Romney, George, Intro. ii. iii. I. LXIX.
Smirke, Robert, R.A. VI. X. XI. XVI. XX. XXIV.-XXX. XXXIII. XLV. XLVI.
Stothard, Thomas, R.A. LXV. LXXXVII.
Tresham, Henry, R.A. XC.
West, Benjamin, President R.A. LXXXIII. LXXXV.
West, Raphael, XXXI.
Westall, Richard, R.A. XLVII. LXVII. LXXVIII. LXXX. XCIV.
Wheatley, Francis, R.A. IV. XXXIV. XXXV. XL.
Wright, Joseph, of Derby, III. XXXIX.
Zucchi. *See* Kauffman.

Sculptors.

Banks, Thomas, R.A. Intro. ii.
Damer, Hon. Anne Seymour, LXXI. XCI.
Roubiliac, Louis Francis, *Frontispiece*.

INTRODUCTION.

The original Series of Engravings from which these Photographic reproductions have been copied was published by John and Josiah Boydell, in the years 1802-4, in two atlas folio volumes, at the cost of Sixty Guineas.

The collection of beautiful pictures long exhibited in London as the Shakespeare Gallery, had their origin, it is said, at a dinner party at Mr. Josiah Boydell's, at West End, Hampstead, in November, 1787, at which a statement was made that, in the opinion of foreigners, the English were unequal to the production of any high-class historical pictures. Alderman Boydell maintained it was otherwise, nothing more being wanted than a suitable subject and adequate encouragement.

A subject was then proposed in Shakespeare's immortal dramatic scenes, the great printseller himself undertaking to give the requisite encouragement. Liberal commissions were given to the first artists of the day,* and the result was the assemblage of the celebrated Shakespeare Gallery in Pall Mall, London, at a cost considerably above one hundred thousand pounds.

Alderman Boydell's career was one memorable as having given, by his liberality, a great impetus to the English school of

---

* Early in 1789, the undertaking was so far advanced that a great number of pictures were painted, and a gallery built on the site of Mr. Dodsley's house in Pall Mall.

engravers. Before his time the art of engraving was at a very low ebb in England; and collectors of prints were in the habit of receiving them from abroad. It may be very justly attributed to the zealous and persevering industry of Mr. Boydell that it was carried to such perfection, as to occasion the works of British engravers to be sought after through every part of Europe, and produced a considerable branch of commerce in objects which had previously been imported. The most comprehensive and magnificent of his speculations was the creation of the Shakespeare Gallery, and the publication of the Series of Prints; as also his folio Edition of Shakespeare.

This Gallery Boydell generously intended to have bequeathed to the Nation, but the interruption of Continental trade, consequent to the wars of the French Revolution, so crippled his resources, that he was compelled to abandon this munificent idea. The following letter, addressed by Alderman Boydell to his friend, Sir John W. Anderson, and read by the latter in the House of Commons, when applying for leave to dispose of the paintings by lottery, fully explains Boydell's reasons, and is also a short outline of his life:—

Cheapside, Feb. 4, 1804.

DEAR SIR,
    The kindness with which you have undertaken to represent my case, calls upon me to lay open to you, with the utmost candour, the circumstances attending it, which I will now endeavour to do as briefly as possible. It is above sixty years since I began to study the art of engraving, in the course of which time, besides employing that long period of life in my profession, with an industry and assiduity that would be improper in me to describe, I have laid out with my brethren, in promoting the commerce of the fine arts in this country, above 350,000*l*. When I first began business, the whole commerce of prints in this country consisted in importing foreign prints, principally from France, to supply the cabinets of the curious in this kingdom. Impressed with the idea that the genius of our own

countrymen, if properly encouraged, was equal to that of foreigners, I set about establishing a *School of Engraving in England;* with what success the public is well acquainted. It is, perhaps, at present sufficient to say, that the whole course of that commerce is changed, very few prints being now imported into this country, while the foreign market is principally supplied with prints from England. In effecting this favourite plan, I have not only spent a long life, but have employed near forty years of the labour of my nephew, Josiah Boydell, who has been bred to the business, and whose assistance during that period has been greatly instrumental in promoting a school of engraving in this country. By the blessing of Providence, these exertions have been very successful; not only in that respect, but in a commercial point of view; for, the large sums I regularly received from the Continent, previous to the French Revolution, for impressions taken from the numerous plates engraved in England, encouraged me to attempt also an *English School of Historical Painting.* I had observed with indignation that the want of such a school had been long made a favourite topic of opprobrium against this country among foreign writers on national taste. No subject, therefore, could be more appropriate for such a national attempt than England's inspired poet, and great painter of nature, Shakespeare; and I flatter myself the most prejudiced foreigner must allow that the Shakespeare Gallery will convince the world that Englishmen want nothing but the fostering hand of encouragement to bring forth their genius in this line of art. I might go further, and defy any of the Italian, Flemish, or French schools to show, in so short a space of time, such an exertion as the Shakespeare Gallery; and if they could have made such an exertion, the pictures would have been marked with all that monotonous sameness which distinguishes those different schools; whereas in the Shakespeare Gallery every artist, partaking of the freedom of his country, and endowed with that originality of thinking so peculiar to its natives, has chosen his own road to what he conceived to be excellence, unshackled by the slavish imitation and uniformity that pervade all the foreign schools. This Gallery I once flattered myself with being able to have left to that generous public who have for so long a period encouraged my undertakings; but unfortunately for those connected with the fine arts, a Vandalic revolution has arisen, which, in convulsing all Europe, has entirely extinguished, except in this happy island, all those who had the taste or the power to promote those arts; while the tyrant that at present governs France, tells that believing and besotted nation, that in the midst of all his robbery and rapine, he is a great patron and promoter of the fine arts; just as if those arts that humanize and polish mankind could be promoted by such means, and by such a man. You will excuse, my dear Sir, I am sure, some warmth in an old man on this subject, when I inform you that this unhappy revolution has cut up by the roots that revenue from the Continent which enabled me to undertake such considerable works in this country. At the same time, as I am laying my case fairly before you, it should not be disguised that my natural enthusiasm for promoting the fine arts (perhaps buoyed up by success), made me improvident; for, had I laid by but ten pounds out of every hundred pounds my plates produced, I should not now have had occasion to trouble my friends, or appeal to the public; but, on the contrary, I flew with impatience to employ some new artist with the whole gains of my former undertakings. I see too late my error; for I have thereby decreased my ready money, and increased my stock of copper-plates to such a size, that all the printsellers in Europe could not purchase it, especially at these times so unfavourable to the arts. Having thus candidly owned my error, I have but one word to say in extenuation. My receipts from abroad had been so large, and continued so regular, that I at all times found them fully adequate to support my undertakings at home. I could not calculate on the present crisis, which has totally annihilated them. I certainly calculated on some defalcation of these receipts by a French or Spanish war, or both; but with France or Spain I carried on but little commerce—Flanders, Holland, and Germany, who, no doubt, supplied the rest of Europe, were the great marts; but alas! they are now no more. The convulsion that has disjointed and ruined the whole Continent I did not foresee—I know no man that did. On that head, therefore, though it has nearly ruined me and mine, I can take but little blame to myself. In this state of things I throw myself with confidence upon that public who has always been but too partial to my poor endeavours, for the disposal of that which, in happier days, I flattered myself to have presented to them. I know of no means by which that can be effected just now but by a lottery; and if the legislature will have the goodness to grant a permission for that purpose, they will at least have the assurance of the even tenour of a long life, that it will be fairly and honourably conducted. The objects of it are my pictures, galleries, drawings, &c., &c., which, unconnected with my copper-plates and trade, are much more than sufficient to pay, if properly disposed of, all I owe in the world. I hope you, my dear Sir, and every honest man, at any age, will feel for my anxiety to discharge my debts, but at my advanced age of eighty-five I feel it becomes doubly desirable.

I am, dear Sir,
With great regard,
Your obedient and obliged Servant,
JOHN BOYDELL.

Alderman John Boydell, who was born in 1719, lived to see every ticket of the lottery disposed of, but not until the prizes were drawn; he died in December, 1804, universally regretted.

The dedication of the two volumes of Prints, to their Majesties, was made by his nephew and partner, Mr. Josiah Boydell, and dated the 25th of March, 1805.

A Medal, struck by Boulton of Birmingham, was presented to each subscriber to the Work—a reduction of which appears on the title-page of this volume.

The prize in the lottery was drawn on the 28th January, 1805, and the fortunate holder of the successful ticket was Mr. Tassie, of Leicester Square.

On the 17th and 18th of May, in the same year, the pictures were sold by Mr. Christie, in separate lots, by which the great collection became scattered. The produce of the sale displayed a striking contrast to the prices which had been paid for the paintings; the sum for which they sold not amounting to much more than six thousand pounds.

That many valuable pictures did not realise higher sums than they were sold for, must be attributed to their being so large ; and for large pictures the apartments of this country are not generally calculated.

To a certain extent the popularity of this magnificent series of prints has been affected by the same reason. Two volumes atlas folio are out of place in all but the libraries of the very rich, and even then so cumbrous and unhandy that they often are disposed of for sheer want of space ; yet seldom has the price been depreciated below ten guineas.

By the aid of photography the whole series, excepting the portraits of their Majesties George III. and Queen Charlotte, is now presented in a handy form, suitable for ordinary libraries or the drawing-room table, and offered as an appropriate memorial of the tercentenary celebration of the poet's birth.

Many series of Shakespeare illustrations may be cited, as that of Mortimer, 1775 ; of Taylor, 1783 and 1792 ; Harding, 1793 ; those illustrating Manley Wood's Edition, 1806 ; Thurston, 1810 ; Rhodes, 1813 ; Heath and Finden, 1825 ; Frank Howard, 1827 ; and in Germany by Retzsch, 1833–47.

Our modern artists have ably illustrated the works of our great dramatist, as the productions of Maclise, Landseer, Leslie, F. Pickersgill, Frith, Le Jeune, Harlow, and others, will amply show ; but no *series* has hitherto been published so magnificent in conception or execution, or so completely the production of the English school, as that which is now reproduced.

The edition of Shakespeare, published by Messrs. Boydell in nine folio volumes, contained 100 other illustrations, which may possibly be undertaken as a fitting companion to this series, should the public encouragement of this reproduction sufficiently warrant further speculation.

1.

THE ALTO-RELIEVO.

IN FRONT OF THE GALLERY, PALL MALL.

This work represents Shakespeare seated on a rock, between the Muses of Poetry and Painting. Poetry is on his right hand, addressing Shakespeare, and presenting him with a wreath of bays, while she celebrates his praise on her lyre. Her head is ornamented with a double mask, to show she has bestowed the double power of Tragedy and Comedy upon her favourite son. Shakespeare is represented as listening to her with pleasure and attention. On his left is Painting, who is addressing the spectator, with one hand extended towards Shakespeare's breast, pointing him out as the proper object of her pencil, while he leans his left hand on her shoulder, as if accepting her assistance.

Sculptured by THOMAS BANKS, R.A.
Engraved by BENJAMIN SMITH.

Introd.   Ph. 1.

2.

THE INFANT SHAKESPEARE ATTENDED BY NATURE AND THE PASSIONS.

Nature is represented with her face unveiled to her favourite child, who is placed between Joy and Sorrow. On the right hand of Nature are Love, Hatred, and Jealousy; on her left hand, Anger, Envy, and Fear.

Painted by GEORGE ROMNEY.
Engraved by BENJAMIN SMITH.

Рис. 2.

xxx

3.

SHAKESPEARE NURSED BY TRAGEDY AND COMEDY.

Shakespeare is here represented by a charming infant, happy with his toy, and unconscious of the marvellous influence which his unthought-of works would have on the Tragic and the Comic Muses who are carefully tending and ministering to his infant wants, anticipating the homage due to him who has been justly termed by Ben Jonson —

" Soule of the Age !
The applause ! delight ! the wonder of our Stage !"

Painted by GEORGE ROMNEY.
Engraved by BENJAMIN SMITH.

Introd. Pl. 3.

THE TEMPEST.

I.

THE TEMPEST.

Act I. Scene 2.

THE ENCHANTED ISLAND: BEFORE THE CELL OF PROSPERO.

Prospero and Miranda. Enter *Ariel*.

Ariel.   Not a soul
But felt a fever of the mad, and play'd
Some tricks of desperation: All but mariners
Plung'd in the foaming brine, and quit the vessel,
Then all a-fire with me: the king's son, Ferdinand,
With hair up-staring (then like reeds, not hair,)
Was the first man that leap'd; cried, 'Hell is empty,
And all the devils are here.'

Painted by GEORGE ROMNEY.
Engraved by BENJAMIN SMITH.

PH. 1.

THE TEMPEST.

(2)

II.

THE TEMPEST.

Act I. Scene 2.

THE ENCHANTED ISLAND: BEFORE THE CELL OF PROSPERO.

Prospero, Miranda, and Ariel. Enter *Caliban.*

Pro. For this, be sure, to-night thou shalt have cramps,
Side-stitches that shall pen thy breath up; urchins
Shall, for that vast of night that they may work,
All exercise on thee: thou shalt be pinch'd
As thick as honeycomb, each pinch more stinging
Than bees that made them.

Painted by HENRY FUSELI, R.A.
Engraved by JOHN PETER SIMON.

Pl. II.

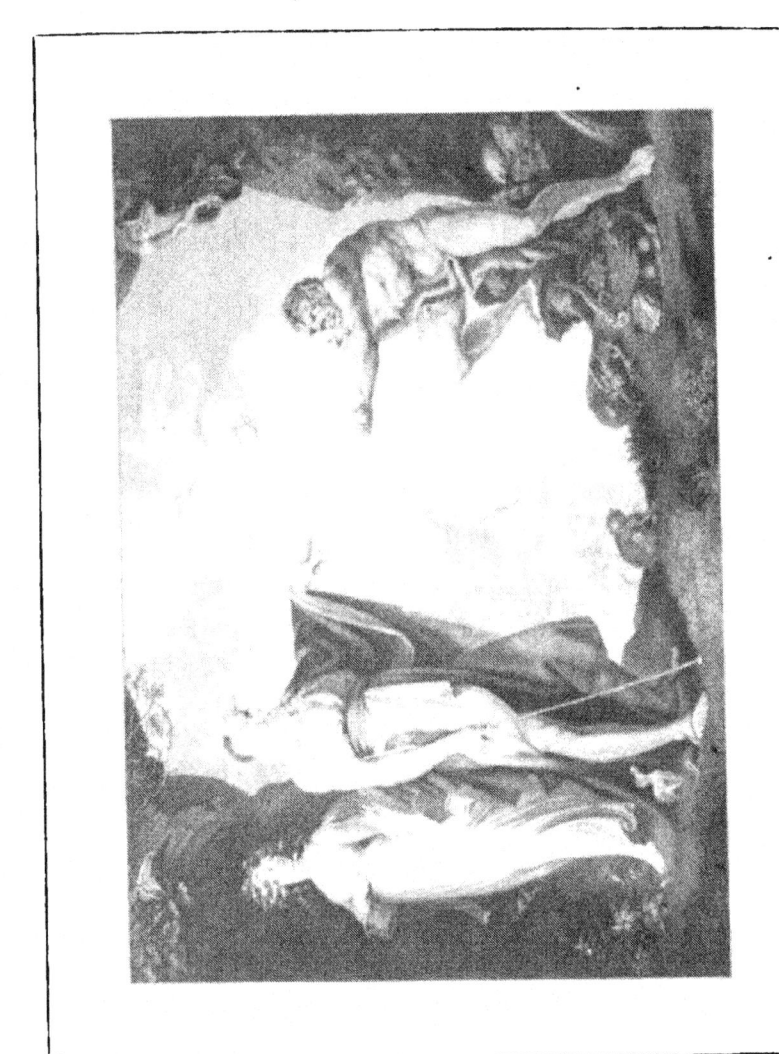

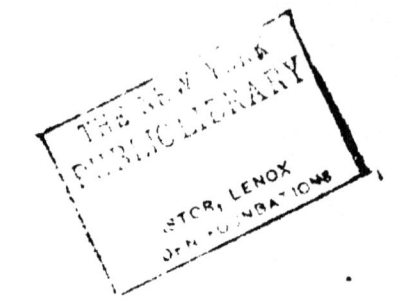

THE TEMPEST.

III.

THE TEMPEST.

Act IV. Scene 1.

PROSPERO'S CELL.

Prospero, Ferdinand, Miranda; a Mask exhibiting, Iris, Ceres, Juno, Nymphs; Caliban, Trinculo, and Stephano, at a distance.

> *Pro.* You do look, my son, in a mov'd sort
> As if you were dismay'd: be cheerful, sir:
> Our revels now are ended: these our actors,
> As I foretold you, were all spirits, and
> Are melted into air, into thin air:
> And, like the baseless fabric of this vision,
> The cloud-capp'd towers, the gorgeous palaces,
> The solemn temples, the great globe itself,
> Yea, all which it inherit, shall dissolve;
> And, like this insubstantial pageant faded,
> Leave not a rack behind: We are such stuff
> As dreams are made on, and our little life
> Is rounded with a sleep.

Painted by JOSEPH WRIGHT.
Engraved by ROBERT THEW.

Рис. III.

THE TEMPEST.

IV.

THE TEMPEST.

Act V. Scene 1.

PROSPERO'S CELL.

The entrance of the Cell opens, and discovers Ferdinand and Miranda playing at Chess.

    Mira. Sweet lord, you play me false.
    Fer.   No, my dearest love,
I would not for the world.
    Mira. Yes, for a score of kingdoms you should wrangle,
And I would call it fair play.

Painted by FRANCIS WHEATLEY, R.A.
Engraved by CAROLINE WATSON.

Рис. IV.

TWO GENTLEMEN OF VERONA.

V.

THE TWO GENTLEMEN OF VERONA.

Act V. Scene 4.

A FOREST.

Valentine, Proteus, Silvia, and Julia.

Val. Ruffian, let go that rude uncivil touch;
Thou friend of an ill fashion!
   Pro.   Valentine!
   Val. Thou common friend, that's without faith or love;
(For such is a friend now;) treacherous man!
Thou hast beguil'd my hopes; nought but mine eye
Could have persuaded me: Now I dare not say
I have one friend alive; thou wouldst disprove me.
Who should be trusted when one's own right hand
Is perjur'd to the bosom? Proteus,
I am sorry I must never trust thee more,
But count the world a stranger for thy sake.
The private wound is deepest: O time most accurs'd!
'Mongst all foes, that a friend should be the worst.

Painted by MARIA ANGELICA KAUFFMAN, R.A.
Engraved by LUIGI SCHIAVONETTI.

Ph. A.

THE MERRY WIVES OF WINDSOR.

(1)

VI.

THE MERRY WIVES OF WINDSOR.

Act I. Scene 1.

BEFORE PAGE'S HOUSE.

Anne Page, Slender, and Simple.

Slen. Mistress Anne, yourself shall go first.
Anne. Not I, sir; pray you, keep on.
Slen. Truly, I will not go first; truly, la: I will not do you that wrong.
Anne. I pray you, sir.
Slen. I'll rather be unmannerly than troublesome; you do yourself wrong, indeed, la.

Painted by ROBERT SMIRKE, R.A.
Engraved by JOHN PETER SIMON.

Pl. VI.

THE
MERRY WIVES
OF
WINDSOR.
(2)

VII.

THE MERRY WIVES OF WINDSOR.

Act II. Scene 1.

BEFORE PAGE'S HOUSE.

Mrs. Page and Mrs. Ford.

Mrs. Ford. Why this is the very same; the very hand, the very words: What doth he think of us?
Mrs. Page. Nay, I know not: It makes me almost ready to wrangle with mine own honesty. I'll entertain myself like one that I am not acquainted withal.

Painted by the Rev. WILLIAM PETERS, R.A.
Engraved by ROBERT THEW.

Рис. VII.

THE
MERRY WIVES
OF
WINDSOR.

(3)

VIII.

THE MERRY WIVES OF WINDSOR.

Act III. Scene 3.

A ROOM IN FORD'S HOUSE.

Mrs. Page, Mrs. Ford, and Falstaff.

Fal. I love thee. Help me away: let me creep in here; I'll never ——
   [*He goes into the basket; they cover him with foul linen.*
Mrs. Page. Help to cover your master, boy: Call your men, mistress Ford:—you dissembling knight!

Painted by the Rev. WILLIAM PETERS, R.A.
Engraved by JOHN PETER SIMON.

Рн. VIII.

THE
MERRY WIVES
OF
WINDSOR.
(4)

IX.

THE MERRY WIVES OF WINDSOR.

Act IV. Scene 2.

A ROOM IN FORD'S HOUSE.

Ford, Shallow, Page, Caius, Sir Hugh Evans, Falstaff, as the old Woman of Brentford, Mrs. Ford, and Mrs. Page.

Mrs. Page. Come, mother Prat, come, give me your hand.
Ford. I'll *prat* her:—Out of my door, you witch, (*beats him*) you rag, you baggage, you polecat, you ronyon! Out! out! I'll conjure you, I'll fortune-tell you.

Painted by JAMES DURNO.
Engraved by THOMAS RYDER.

Pl. IX.

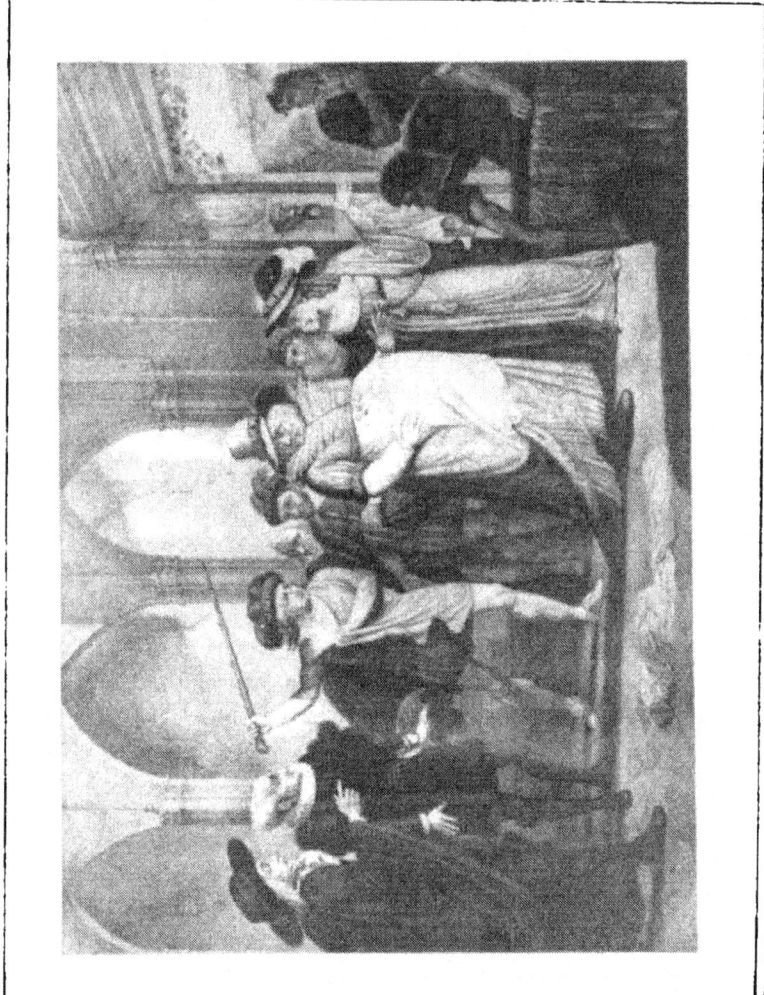

THE MERRY WIVES OF WINDSOR.

(5)

X.

THE MERRY WIVES OF WINDSOR.

Act V. Scene 5.

WINDSOR PARK.

Falstaff (disguised with a Buck's Head on), Fairies, Mrs. Ford, Mrs. Page, Mrs. Quickly, Pistol, Sir Hugh Evans, Fenton, and Anne Page.

    Quick. With trial-fire touch me his finger-end.
If he be chaste, the flame will back descend
And turn him to no pain; but if he start,
It is the flesh of a corrupted heart.
    Pist. A trial, come.
    Eva.   Come, will this wood take fire?
                                  [*They burn him with their tapers.*
    Fal. Oh, oh, oh!
    Quick. Corrupt, corrupt, and tainted in desire!
About him, fairies; sing a scornful rhyme;
And, as you trip, still pinch him to your time.

Painted by Robert Smirke, R.A.
Engraved by Isaac Taylor, Jun.

PL. X.

MEASURE
FOR
MEASURE.

(1)

XI.

MEASURE FOR MEASURE.

Act II. Scene 1.

ANGELO'S HOUSE.

Escalus, a Justice, Elbow, Froth, Clown, Officers, and others.

Escal. Truly, officer, because he hath some offences in him that thou wouldst discover if thou couldst, let him continue in his courses, till thou know'st what they are.

Elb. Marry, I thank your worship for it:—Thou seest, thou wicked varlet now, what's come upon thee; thou art to continue now, thou varlet; thou art to continue.

Painted by ROBERT SMIRKE, R.A.
Engraved by THOMAS RYDER *and* C. G. PLAYTER.

Pl. XI.

MEASURE FOR MEASURE.

(2)

XII.

MEASURE FOR MEASURE.

Act V. Scene 1.

A PUBLIC PLACE NEAR THE CITY GATE.

The Duke in a Friar's habit, Varrius, Lords, Angelo, Escalus, Lucio, and Citizens. Isabella, Peter, Mariana, Provost, &c.

Lucio. Come, sir; come, sir; come, sir; foh, sir: Why, you bald-pated, lying rascal! you must be hooded, must you? Show your knave's visage, ——— ——— show your sheep-biting face, and be hanged an hour! Will't not off?
  [*Pulls off the Friar's hood, and discovers the Duke.*

Duke. Thou art the first knave that e'er made a duke.—
First, provost, let me bail these gentle three:—
Sneak not away, sir; [*to Lucio*] for the friar and you
Must have a word anon:— lay hold on him.

Painted by THOMAS KIRK.
Engraved by PETER SIMON.

Pl. XII.

THE
COMEDY
OF
ERRORS.

XIII.

THE COMEDY OF ERRORS.

Act V. Scene 1.

A STREET BEFORE THE PRIORY.

Merchant, Angelo, Lady Abbess, Adriana, Courtezan, Duke, Ægeon, Antipholus and Dromio of Syracuse, Antipholus and Dromio of Ephesus, Headsman, &c.

 Abbess. Most mighty Duke, behold a man much wrong'd.
         [*All gather to see him.*
 Adr. I see two husbands, or mine eyes deceive me.
 Duke. One of these men is genius to the other;
And so of these: Which is the natural man,
And which the spirit? Who deciphers them?
 Dro. S. I, sir, am Dromio; command him away.
 Dro. E. I, sir, am Dromio; pray, let me stay.
 Ant. S. Ægeon, art thou not? or else his ghost?
 Dro. S. O, my old master, who hath bound him here?

   Painted by JOHN FRANCIS RIGAUD, R.A.
   Engraved by C. G. PLAYTER.

PH. XIII.

MUCH ADO ABOUT NOTHING.

(1)

XIV.

MUCH ADO ABOUT NOTHING.

Act III. Scene 1.

AN ORCHARD.

Hero, Ursula, and Beatrice.

Hero. Then go we near her, that her ear lose nothing
Of the false sweet bait that we lay for it.—
                      [*They advance to the bower.*
No, truly, Ursula, she is too disdainful;
I know, her spirits are as coy and wild
As haggards of the rock.
    Urs.   But are you sure,
That Benedick loves Beatrice so entirely?

Painted by the Rev. WILLIAM PETERS, R.A.
Engraved by PETER SIMON.

Ph. XIV.

MUCH ADO ABOUT NOTHING.

XV.

MUCH ADO ABOUT NOTHING.

Act IV. Scene 1.

THE INSIDE OF A CHURCH.

Don Pedro, Don John, Leonato, Friar, Claudio, Benedick, Hero, and Beatrice.

Claud. O Hero! what a Hero hadst thou been,
If half thy outward graces had been placed
About thy thoughts, and counsels of thy heart!
But, fare thee well, most foul, most fair! farewell,
Thou pure impiety, and impious purity!
For thee I'll lock up all the gates of love,
And on my eyelids shall conjecture hang,
To turn all beauty into thoughts of harm,
And never shall it more be gracious.
  Leon. Hath no man's dagger here a point for me?
            [*Hero swoons.*
  Beat. Why, how now, cousin? wherefore sink you down?
  D. John. Come, let us go: these things, come thus to light,
Smother her spirits up.

Painted by WILLIAM HAMILTON, R.A.
Engraved by PETER SIMON.

Pl. XV.

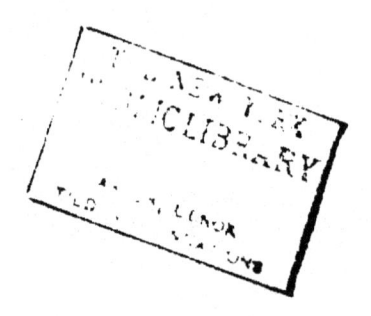

MUCH ADO
ABOUT
NOTHING.

XVI.

MUCH ADO ABOUT NOTHING.

Act IV. Scene 2.

A PRISON.

Dogberry, Verges, Boracchio, Conrade, the Town Clerk, and Sexton.

Sexton. What heard you him say else?
2 *Watch.* Marry, that he had received a thousand ducats of don John, for accusing the lady Hero wrongfully.
Dogb. Flat burglary, as ever was committed.
Verg. Yea, by the mass, that it is.
Sexton. What else, fellow?
1 *Watch.* And that count Claudio did mean, upon his words, to disgrace Hero before the whole assembly, and not marry her.
Dogb. O villain! thou wilt be condemned into everlasting redemption for this.
Sexton. What else?
2 *Watch.* This is all.

Painted by ROBERT SMIRKE, R.A.
Engraved by JOHN OGBORNE.

Ph. XVI.

THE NEW YORK
PUBLIC LIBRARY

ASTOR, LENOX
TILDEN FOUNDATIONS

LOVE'S
LABOUR'S
LOST.

XVII.

LOVE'S LABOUR'S LOST.

Act IV. Scene 1.

A PAVILION IN THE PARK, NEAR THE PALACE.

Princess, Rosaline, Maria, Katharine, Lords, Attendants, and a Forester.

 Prin. Was that the king, that spurr'd his horse so hard
Against the steep uprising of the hill?
 Boyet. I know not; but, I think, it was not he.
 Prin. Whoe'er he was, he show'd a mounting mind.
Well, lords, to-day we shall have our despatch;
On Saturday we will return to France.—
Then, forester, my friend, where is the bush,
That we must stand and play the murderer in?
 For. Here by, upon the edge of yonder coppice;
A stand, where you may make the fairest shoot.

Painted by WILLIAM HAMILTON, R.A.
Engraved by THOMAS RYDER.

PH. XVII.

A MIDSUMMER-
NIGHT'S
DREAM.

XVIII.

A MIDSUMMER-NIGHT'S DREAM.

Act IV. Scene 1.

A WOOD.

Titania, Queen of the Fairies, Bottom, Fairies attending, &c. &c.

Bot. Scratch my head, Peas-blossom.—Where's monsieur Cobweb?

Cob. Ready.

Bot. Monsieur Cobweb; good monsieur, get your weapons in your hand, and kill me a red-hipped humble-bee on the top of a thistle; and good monsieur, bring me the honey-bag. Do not fret yourself too much in the action, monsieur; and, good monsieur, have a care the honey-bag break not; I would be loth to have you overflown with a honey-bag, signior.—Where's monsieur Mustard-seed?

Must. Ready.

Bot. Give me your neif, monsieur Mustard-seed. Pray you, leave your courtesy, good monsieur.

Must. What's your will?

Bot. Nothing, good monsieur, but to help cavalero Cobweb to scratch. I must to the barber's, monsieur; for, methinks, I am marvellous hairy about the face; and I am such a tender ass, if my hair do but tickle me I must scratch.

Painted by HENRY FUSELI, R.A.
Engraved by JOHN PETER SIMON.

Pl. XVIII.

A
MIDSUMMER-
NIGHT'S
DREAM.

(2)

XIX.

A MIDSUMMER-NIGHT'S DREAM.

Act IV. Scene 1.

A WOOD.

Oberon, Queen of the Fairies, Puck, Bottom, Fairies attending, &c.

   Tita. My Oberon! what visions have I seen!
Methought I was enamour'd of an ass.
   Obe. There lies your love.
   Tita. How came these things to pass?
O, how mine eyes do loath his visage now!
   Obe. Silence a while.—Robin, take off this head.—
Titania, music call; and strike more dead
Than common sleep, of all these five the sense.

Painted by HENRY FUSELI, R.A.
Engraved by THOMAS RYDER.

Pl. XIX.

THE
MERCHANT
OF
VENICE.

(1)

XX.

THE MERCHANT OF VENICE.

Act II. Scene 5.

SHYLOCK'S HOUSE.

Shylock, Jessica, and Launcelot.

Shy. What! are there masques? Hear you me, Jessica:
Lock up my doors; and when you hear the drum,
And the vile squealing of the wry-neck'd fife,
Clamber not you up to the casements then,
Nor thrust your head into the public street,
To gaze on Christian fools with varnish'd faces:
But stop my house's ears, I mean my casements;
Let not the sound of shallow foppery enter
My sober house.—

Painted by Robert Smirke, R.A.
Engraved by John Peter Simon.

Рн. XX.

THE NEW YORK
PUBLIC LIBRARY

ASTOR, LENOX
TILDEN FOUNDATIONS

THE
MERCHANT
OF
VENICE.

(2)

XXI.

THE MERCHANT OF VENICE.

Act V. Scene 1.

BELMONT: A GROVE OR GREEN PLACE BEFORE PORTIA'S HOUSE.

Jessica, Lorenzo, and Stephano.

How sweet the moon-light sleeps upon this bank!
Here will we sit, and let the sounds of music
Creep in our ears; soft stillness, and the night,
Become the touches of sweet harmony.
Sit, Jessica. Look how the floor of heaven
Is thick inlaid with patines of bright gold.
There's not the smallest orb which thou behold'st
But in his motion like an angel sings,
Still quiring to the young-eyed cherubins:
Such harmony is in immortal souls;
But whilst this muddy vesture of decay
Doth grossly close it in, we cannot hear it.—

Painted by WILLIAM HODGES, R.A.
Engraved by JOHN BROWNE.

PL. XXI.

AS YOU
LIKE IT.

(1)

XXII.

AS YOU LIKE IT.

Act I. Scene 2.

BEFORE THE DUKE'S PALACE.

---

*Rosalind, Celia, Orlando, Duke, and attendants.
Charles carried off.*

Ros.   Gentleman,
              [*Giving him a chain from her neck.*
Wear this for me,—one out of suits with fortune,
That could give more but that her hand lacks means.

Painted by J. DOWNMAN, R.A.
Engraved by W. LENEY.

PH. XXII.

AS YOU LIKE IT.

XXIII.

AS YOU LIKE IT.

Act II. Scene 1.

THE FOREST OF ARDEN.

Jaques, Amiens, and the First Lord.

1 *Lord.* To-day, my lord of Amiens and myself
Did steal behind him, as he lay along
Under an oak, whose antique roots peep out
Upon the brook that brawls along this wood:
To the which place a poor sequester'd stag,
That from the hunters' aim had ta'en a hurt,
Did come to languish; and, indeed, my lord,
The wretched animal heav'd forth such groans,
That their discharge did stretch his leathern coat
Almost to bursting; and the big round tears
Cours'd one another down his innocent nose
In piteous chase: and thus the hairy fool,
Much marked of the melancholy Jaques,
Stood on the extremest verge of the swift brook,
Augmenting it with tears.

Painted by WILLIAM HODGES, R.A.
Engraved by SAMUEL MIDDIMAN.

Pл. XXIII.

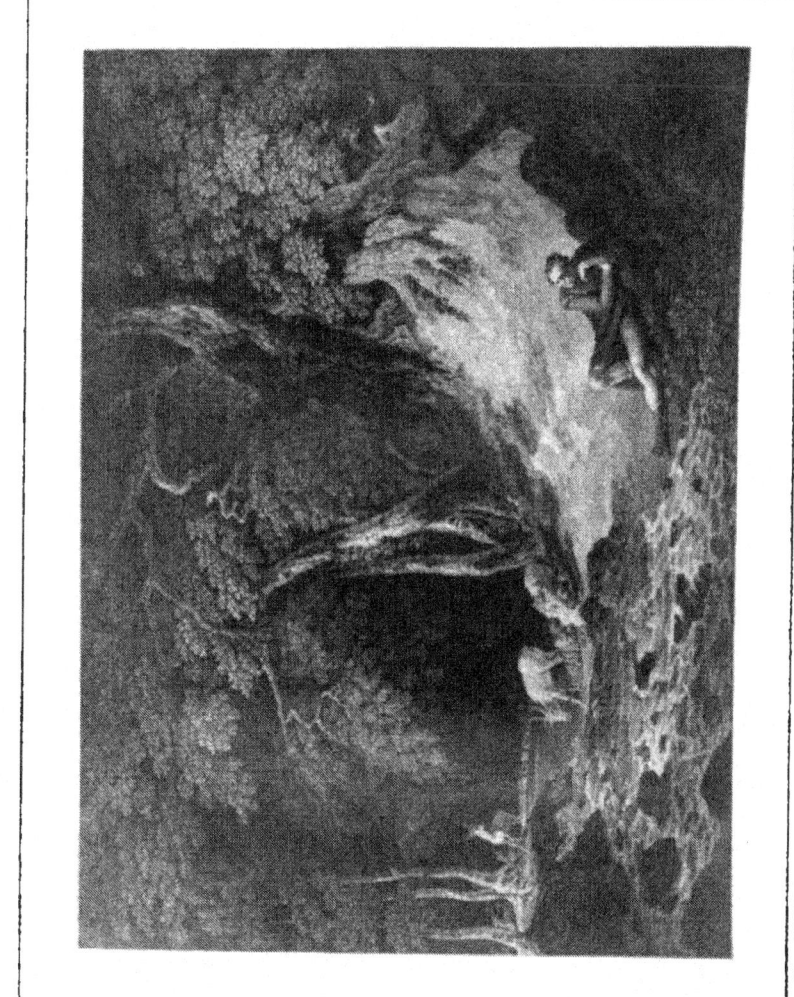

AS YOU LIKE IT.

XXIV.

AS YOU LIKE IT.

Act II. Scene 7.

THE FOREST OF ARDEN.

Duke, Amiens, Jaques, and others.

(THE SEVEN AGES OF MAN—FIRST AGE.)

Jaq.   At first, the infant,
Mewling and puking in the nurse's arms.

Painted by ROBERT SMIRKE, R.A.
Engraved by PELTRO WILLIAM TOMKINS.

PH. XXIV.

AS YOU LIKE IT.

XXV.

AS YOU LIKE IT.

Act II. Scene 7.

THE FOREST OF ARDEN.

Duke, Amiens, Jaques, and others.

(THE SEVEN AGES OF MAN—SECOND AGE.)

Jaq. Then the whining schoolboy, with his satchel,
And shining morning face, creeping like snail
Unwillingly to school.

Painted by ROBERT SMIRKE, R.A.
Engraved by JOHN OGBORNE.

Pl. XXV

THE NEW YORK
PUBLIC LIBRARY

ASTOR, LENOX
TILDEN FOUNDATIONS

AS YOU LIKE IT.

XXVI.

AS YOU LIKE IT.

Act II. Scene 7.

THE FOREST OF ARDEN.

Duke, Amiens, Jaques, and others.

(THE SEVEN AGES OF MAN—THIRD AGE.)

Jaq. ——— And then, the lover,
Sighing like furnace, with a woeful ballad
Made to his mistress' eyebrow.

Painted by ROBERT SMIRKE, R.A.
Engraved by ROBERT THEW.

Pl. XXVI.

AS YOU LIKE IT.

XXVII.

AS YOU LIKE IT.

Act II. Scene 7.

THE FOREST OF ARDEN.

Duke, Amiens, Jaques, and others.

(THE SEVEN AGES OF MAN — FOURTH AGE.)

Jaq.   Then, a soldier;
Full of strange oaths, and bearded like the pard,
Jealous in honour, sudden and quick in quarrel,
Seeking the bubble reputation
Even in the cannon's mouth.

Painted by ROBERT SMIRKE, R.A.
Engraved by JOHN OGBORNE.

Pl. XXVII.

AS YOU
LIKE IT.

(7)

XXVIII.

AS YOU LIKE IT.

Act II. Scene 7.

THE FOREST OF ARDEN.

Duke, Amiens, Jaques, and others.

(THE SEVEN AGES OF MAN—FIFTH AGE.)

 Jaq. —— And then, the justice;
In fair round belly, with good capon lin'd,
With eyes severe, and beard of formal cut,
Full of wise saws and modern instances,
And so he plays his part.

Painted by ROBERT SMIRKE, R.A.
Engraved by JOHN PETER SIMON.

Pl. XXVIII.

AS YOU
LIKE IT.

XXIX.

AS YOU LIKE IT.

Act II. Scene 7.

THE FOREST OF ARDEN.

Duke, Amiens, Jaques, and others.

(THE SEVEN AGES OF MAN—SIXTH AGE.)

Jaq.   The sixth age shifts
Into the lean and slipper'd pantaloon;
With spectacles on nose, and pouch on side;
His youthful hose well sav'd, a world too wide
For his shrunk shank; and his big manly voice,
Turning again toward childish treble, pipes
And whistles in his sound.

Painted by ROBERT SMIRKE, R.A.
Engraved by W. LENEY.

PL. XXIX.

THE NEW YORK
PUBLIC LIBRARY

ASTOR, LENOX
TILDEN FOUNDATIONS

AS YOU
LIKE IT.
—
(B)

XXX.

AS YOU LIKE IT.

Act II. Scene 7.

THE FOREST OF ARDEN.

Duke, Amiens, Jaques, and others.

(THE SEVEN AGES OF MAN — THE LAST.)

Jaq.   Last scene of all,
That ends this strange eventful history,
Is second childishness, and mere oblivion ;
Sans teeth, sans eyes, sans taste, sans everything.

Painted by ROBERT SMIRKE, R.A.
Engraved by JOHN PETER SIMON.

Ph. XXX.

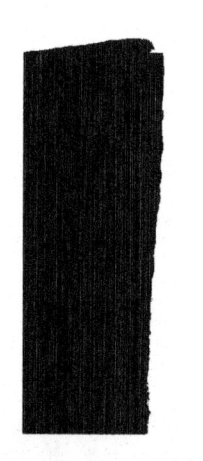

AS YOU
LIKE IT.

(10)

XXXI.

AS YOU LIKE IT.

Act IV. Scene 3.

A FOREST.

Orlando and Oliver.

Oli. Under an old oak, whose boughs were moss'd with age,
And high top bald with dry antiquity,
A wretched ragged man, o'ergrown with hair,
Lay sleeping on his back: about his neck
A green and gilded snake had wreath'd itself,
Who with her head, nimble in threats, approach'd
The opening of his mouth; but suddenly
Seeing Orlando, it unlink'd itself,
And with indented glides did slip away
Into a bush: under which bush's shade
A lioness, with udders all drawn dry,
Lay couching, head on ground, with catlike watch,
When that the sleeping man should stir; for 't is
The royal disposition of that beast,
To prey on nothing that doth seem as dead;
This seen, Orlando did approach the man,
And found it was his brother, his elder brother.

Painted by RAPHAEL WEST.
Engraved by W. C. WILSON.

Pl. XXXI.

AS YOU LIKE IT.

XXXII.

AS YOU LIKE IT.

Act V. Scene 4.

A FOREST.

Duke Senior, Amiens, Jaques, Orlando, Oliver, Celia, Rosalind, Audrey, Clown, Silvius, Phebe, Hymen, &c.

Ros. To you I give myself, for I am yours.
            [*To Duke Senior.*
To you I give myself, for I am yours.
            [*To Orlando.*

Painted by WILLIAM HAMILTON, R.A.
Engraved by PETER SIMON.

Pl. XXXII.

THE
PUBLIC LIBRARY
ASTOR, LENOX
TILDEN FOUNDATIONS

THE TAMING OF THE SHREW.

XXXIII

THE TAMING OF THE SHREW.

Induction. Scene 4.

A ROOM IN THE LORD'S HOUSE.

Sly, with Lord and Attendants; some with apparel, bason and ewer, and other appurtenances.

Sly. Am I a lord? and have I such a lady?
Or do I dream, or have I dream'd till now?
I do not sleep: I see, I hear, I speak;
I smell sweet savours, and I feel soft things:—
Upon my life, I am a lord, indeed;
And not a tinker, nor Christophero Sly.
Well, bring our lady hither to our sight;
And once again, a pot o' the smallest ale.

Painted by ROBERT SMIRKE, R.A.
Engraved by ROBERT THEW.

Pl. XXXIII.

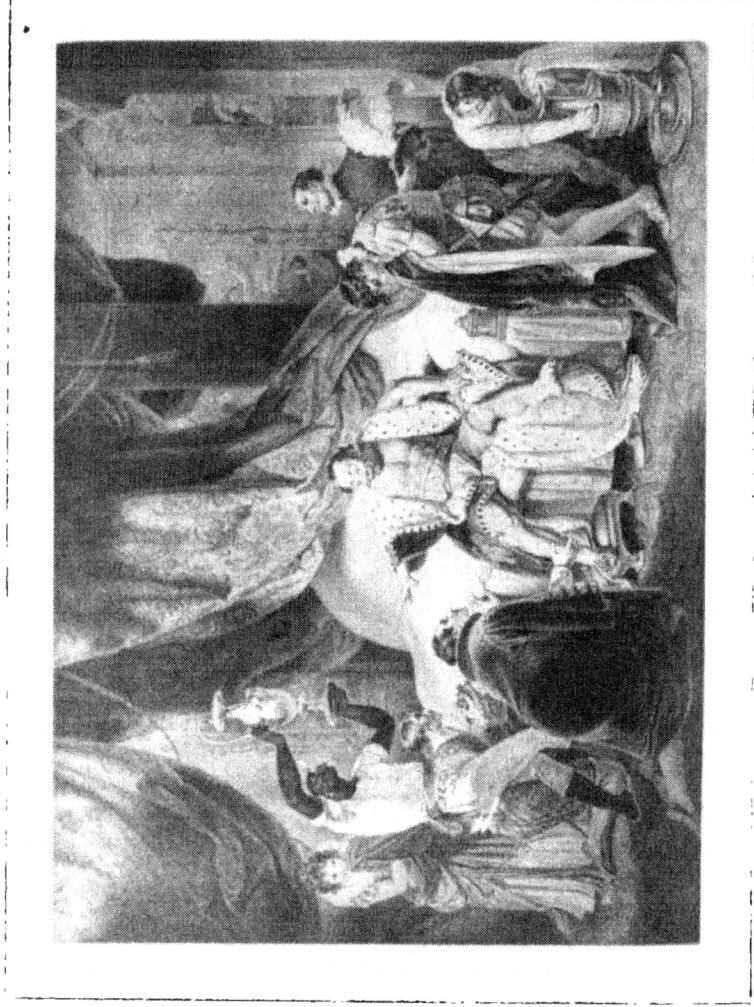

THE TAMING OF THE SHREW.

(2)

XXXIV.

THE TAMING OF THE SHREW.

Act III. Scene 2.

BAPTISTA'S HOUSE.

---

*Petruchio, Katharina, Bianca, Hortensia, Baptista, Grumio,
and Train.*

   Pet. But for my bonny Kate, she must with me.
Nay, look not big, nor stamp, nor stare, nor fret;
I will be master of what is mine own:
She is my goods, my chattels; she is my house,
My household-stuff, my field, my barn,
My horse, my ox, my ass, my anything;
And here she stands, touch her whoever dare;
I'll bring mine action on the proudest he
That stops my way in Padua. Grumio,
Draw forth thy weapon, we are beset with thieves;
Rescue thy mistress, if thou be a man:—
Fear not, sweet wench, they shall not touch thee, Kate;
I'll buckler thee against a million.

Painted by FRANCIS WHEATLEY, R.A.
Engraved by JOHN PETER SIMON.

Pl. XXXIV.

ALL'S WELL THAT ENDS WELL.

XXXV.

ALL'S WELL THAT ENDS WELL.

Act V. Scene 3.

A ROOM IN THE COUNTESS'S PALACE.

King, Countess, Lafeu, Lords, Attendants, &c. Bertram guarded,
Helena, Diana, and Widow.

Hel. O, my good lord, when I was like this maid,
I found you wond'rous kind. There is your ring,
And, look you, here's your letter.

Painted by FRANCIS WHEATLEY, R.A.
Engraved by GEORGE SIGMUND *and* JOHN GOTTLIEB FACIUS.

Рис. XXXV.

TWELFTH NIGHT.

(1)

XXXVI.

TWELFTH NIGHT.

Act III. Scene 4.

OLIVIA'S HOUSE.

Olivia, Maria, and Malvolio.

Mal. Sweet lady, ho, ho.

[*Smiles fantastically.*

Oli. Smilest thou?
I sent for thee upon a sad occasion.

Mal. Sad, lady? I could be sad: This does make some obstruction in the blood, this cross-gartering. But what of that? if it please the eye of one, it is with me as the very true sonnet is: 'Please one, and please all.'

Painted by JOHN HENRY RAMBERG.
Engraved by THOMAS RYDER.

Рис. XXXVI.

TWELFTH NIGHT.

(2)

XXXVII.

TWELFTH NIGHT.

Act V. Scene 1.

THE STREET.

The Duke, Viola, Antonio, Officers, Olivia, Priest, and Attendants.

Oli. Father, I charge thee, by thy reverence,
Here to unfold (though lately we intended
To keep in darkness what occasion now
Reveals before 't is ripe) what thou dost know,
Hath newly pass'd between this youth and me.

Painted by WILLIAM HAMILTON, R.A.
Engraved by FRANCESCO BARTOLOZZI, R.A.

Pl. XXXXVII.

THE
WINTER'S
TALE.

(1)

XXXVIII.

THE WINTER'S TALE.

Act II. Scene 3.

A PALACE.

Leontes, Antigonus, Lords, Attendants, and the Infant Perdita.

   Leon. It shall be possible: Swear by this sword,
Thou wilt perform my bidding.
   Ant.   I will, my lord.
   Leon. Mark, and perform it; (seest thou?) for the fail
Of any point in't shall not only be
Death to thyself, but to thy lewd-tongued wife;
Whom, for this time, we pardon. We enjoin thee,
As thou art liegeman to us, that thou carry
This female bastard hence; and that thou bear it
To some remote and desert place, quite out
Of our dominions; and that there thou leave it,
Without more mercy, to its own protection,
And the favour of the climate.

Painted by JOHN OPIE, R.A.
Engraved by JOHN PETER SIMON.

Pl. XXXVIII.

THE NEW YORK
PUBLIC LIBRARY
ASTOR, LENOX
TILDEN FOUNDATIONS

THE
WINTER'S
TALE.
—
(2)

XXXIX.

THE WINTER'S TALE.

Act III. Scene 3.

A DESERT PLACE NEAR THE SEA.

Antigonus pursued by a bear. Shepherd, and Clown.

Clo. I have seen two such sights, by sea, and by land;—but I am not to say, it is a sea, for it is now the sky; betwixt the firmament and it you cannot thrust a bodkin's point.

Shep. Why, boy, how is it?

Clo. I would you did but see how it chafes, how it rages, how it takes up the shore! but that's not to the point! O, the most piteous cry of the poor souls! sometimes to see 'em, and not to see 'em: now the ship boring the moon with her main-mast; and anon swallowed with yest and froth, as you'd thrust a cork into a hogshead. And then for the land-service,—To see how the bear tore out his shoulder-bone; how he cried to me for help, and said his name was Antigonus, a nobleman:—But to make an end of the ship:—to see how the sea flap-dragoned it:—but, first, how the poor souls roared, and the sea mocked them;—and how the poor gentleman roared, and the bear mocked him, both roaring louder than the sea, or weather.

Painted by JOSEPH WRIGHT.
Engraved by SAMUEL MIDDEMAN.

Pl. XXXIX.

THE
WINTER'S
TALE.

(3)

XL.

THE WINTER'S TALE.

Act IV. Scene 3.

A SHEPHERD'S COT.

---

*Florizel, Perdita, Shepherd, Clown, Mopsa, Dorcas, Servants;
Polixenes and Camillo, disguised.*

   Per.   Sir, welcome!
                          [*To Polixenes.*
It is my father's will I should take on me
The hostess-ship o' the day:—You're welcome, sir!
                          [*To Camillo.*
Give me those flowers there, Dorcas.—Reverend sirs,
For you there's rosemary, and rue; these keep
Seeming, and savour, all the winter long:
Grace, and remembrance, be to you both,
And welcome to our shearing!

          Painted by FRANCIS WHEATLEY, R.A.
          Engraved by JAMES FITTLER.

PH. XL.

THE
WINTER'S
TALE.

(4)

XLI.

THE WINTER'S TALE.

Act V. Scene 3.

PAULINA'S HOUSE.

Leontes, Polixenes, Florizel, Perdita, Camillo, Paulina, Lords, and Attendants. Hermione as a statue.

Paul.   Music; awake her: strike.—
                              [*Music.*
'T is time; descend; be stone no more: approach;
Strike all that look upon with marvel.   Come;
I'll fill your grave up: stir; nay, come away;
Bequeath to death your numbness, for from him
Dear life redeems you.— You perceive she stirs;
            [*Hermione comes down from the pedestal.*
Start not: her actions shall be holy, as,
You hear, my spell is lawful; do not shun her,
Until you see her die again; for then
You kill her double : Nay, present your hand:
When she was young you woo'd her; now, in age,
Is she become the suitor!

Painted by WILLIAM HAMILTON, R.A.

Engraved by ROBERT THEW.

Pl. XLIX.

KING JOHN.

XLII.

KING JOHN.

Act IV. Scene 1.

A ROOM IN THE CASTLE OF NORTHAMPTON.

Arthur, Hubert, and Attendants.

Arth. O, save me, Hubert, save me! my eyes are out,
Even with the fierce looks of these bloody men.
  Hub. Give me the iron, I say, and bind him here.
  Arth. Alas, what need you be so boist'rous-rough?
I will not struggle, I will stand stone-still.
For heaven sake, Hubert, let me not be bound!
Nay, hear me, Hubert! drive these men away,
And I will sit as quiet as a lamb;
I will not stir, nor wince, nor speak a word,
Nor look upon the iron angerly:
Thrust but these men away, and I'll forgive you,
Whatever torment you do put me to.

Painted by JAMES NORTHCOTE, R.A.
Engraved by ROBERT THEW.

Pl. XLII.

KING
RICHARD II.
———
(1)

XLIII.

KING RICHARD THE SECOND.

Act IV. Scene 1.

PARLIAMENT HOUSE.

King Richard, Bolingbroke, York, Aumerle, Northumberland, Percy, Fitzwater, Surrey, Bishop of Carlisle, Abbot of Westminster, Herald, &c. and Bagot.

 Boling. Are you contented to resign the crown?
 K. Rich. Ay, no;—no, ay; for I must nothing be;
Therefore no, no, for I resign to thee.
Now mark me how I will undo myself:—
I give this heavy weight from off my head,
And this unwieldy sceptre from my hand,
The pride of kingly sway from out my heart;
With mine own tears I wash away my balm,
With mine own hands I give away my crown,
With mine own tongue deny my sacred state,
With mine own breath release all duteous oaths:
All pomp and majesty I do forswear;
My manors, rents, revenues, I forego;
My acts, decrees, and statutes, I deny:
God pardon all oaths that are broke to me!
God keep all vows unbroke are made to thee!—

Painted by MATHER BROWNE.
Engraved by BENJAMIN SMITH.

Pн. XLIII.

KING RICHARD II.

(2)

XLIV.

KING RICHARD THE SECOND.

Act V. Scene 2.

LONDON; A ROOM IN THE DUKE OF YORK'S PALACE.

The Entrance of King Richard and Bolingbroke into London, as described by the Duke of York.

    York. Then, as I said, the duke, great Bolingbroke,
Mounted upon a hot and fiery steed,
Which his aspiring rider seem'd to know,
With slow, but stately pace, kept on his course,
While all tongues cried—God save thee, Bolingbroke!
You would have thought the very windows spake,
So many greedy looks of young and old
Through casements darted their desiring eyes
Upon his visage; and that all the walls,
With painted imagery, had said at once,—
Jesu preserve thee! welcome, Bolingbroke!
Whilst he, from one side to the other turning,
Bare-headed, lower than his proud steed's neck,
Bespake them thus,—I thank you, countrymen:
And thus still doing, thus he pass'd along.

Painted by JAMES NORTHCOTE, R.A.
Engraved by ROBERT THEW.

Pl. XLIV.

KING
HENRY IV.
PART I.

XLV.

THE FIRST PART OF
KING HENRY THE FOURTH.

Act II. Scene 2.

THE ROAD TO GADSHILL.

Prince Henry, Poins, Peto, Falstaff, Gadshill, Bardolph.

Fal. Come, my masters, let us share, and then to horse before day. An the prince and Poins be not two arrant cowards, there's no equity stirring: there's no more valour in that Poins than in a wild duck.

P. Hen. Your money.
[*Rushing out upon them.*
Poins. Villains.
[*As they are sharing, the Prince and Poins set upon them. They all run away; and Falstaff, after a blow or two, runs away too, leaving the booty behind.*

Painted by ROBERT SMIRKE, R.A. *and* JOSEPH FARINGTON, R.A.
Engraved by SAMUEL MIDDEMAN.

Рис. XLV.

KING
HENRY IV.
PART I.

(2)

XLVI.

THE FIRST PART OF
KING HENRY THE FOURTH.

Act II. Scene 4.

THE BOAR'S-HEAD TAVERN, EASTCHEAP.

Prince Henry, Falstaff, Poins, &c.

Fal. ———— There is a thing, Harry, which thou hast often heard of, and it is known to many in our land by the name of pitch: this pitch, as ancient writers do report, doth defile; so doth the company thou keepest: for, Harry, now I do not speak to thee in drink, but in tears; not in pleasure, but in passion; not in words only, but in woes also:—And yet there is a virtuous man, whom I have often noted in thy company, but I know not his name.

P. Hen. What manner of man, an it like your majesty?

Fal. A good portly man, i' faith, and a corpulent; of a cheerful look, a pleasing eye, and a most noble carriage; and, as I think, his age some fifty, or, by 'r-lady, inclining to threescore; and now I remember me, his name is Falstaff: if that man should be lewdly given, he deceives me; for, Harry, I see virtue in his looks.

Painted by ROBERT SMIRKE, R.A.
Engraved by ROBERT THEW.

Pʜ. XLVI.

KING
HENRY IV.
PART I.
—
(8)

XLVII.

THE FIRST PART OF
KING HENRY THE FOURTH.

Act III. Scene 1.

THE ARCHDEACON OF BANGOR'S HOUSE, IN WALES.

Hotspur, Worcester, Mortimer, and Owen Glendower.

   Wor. Yea, but a little charge will trench him here,
And on this north side win this cape of land;
And then he runs straight and even.
   Hot. I'll have it so; a little charge will do it.
   Glend. I will not have it alter'd.
   Hot.   Will not you?
   Glend. No, nor you shall not.
   Hot.   Who shall say me nay?
   Glend. Why, that will I.
   Hot.   Let me not understand you then;
Speak it in Welsh.

Painted by RICHARD WESTALL, R.A.
Engraved by JOHN PETER SIMON.

PH. XLVII.

KING HENRY IV.
PART I.
(4)

XLVIII.

THE FIRST PART OF

KING HENRY THE FOURTH.

Act V. Scene 4.

PLAIN NEAR SHREWSBURY.

Prince Henry, Hotspur, and Falstaff.

Hot. O, Harry, thou hast robb'd me of my youth:
I better brook the loss of brittle life
Than those proud titles thou hast won of me;
They wound my thoughts worse than the sword my flesh:—
But thought 's the slave of life, and life time's fool;
And time, that takes survey of all the world,
Must have a stop. O, I could prophesy,
But that the earthy and cold hand of death
Lies on my tongue: No, Percy, thou art dust,
And food for ——   [*Dies.*
 P. Hen. For worms, brave Percy: Fare thee well, great
   heart!—

Painted by JOHN FRANCIS RIGAUD, R.A.
Engraved by THOMAS RYDER.

PH. XLVIII.

THE NEW YORK
PUBLIC LIBRARY

ASTOR, LENOX
TILDEN FOUNDATIONS

KING HENRY IV.
PART II.

XLVIII.*

THE SECOND PART OF

KING HENRY THE FOURTH.

Act II. Scene 4.

ROOM IN THE BOAR'S HEAD TAVERN, EASTCHEAP.

---

*Doll Tearsheet and Falstaff.   Prince Henry and Poins;
disguised like Drawers.*

Fal. Thou dost give me flattering busses.
Doll. Nay, truly; I kiss thee with a most constant heart.
Fal. I am old, I am old.
Doll. I love thee better than I love e'er a scurvy young boy of them all.
Fal. What stuff wilt thou have a kirtle of? I shall receive money on Thursday; thou shalt have a cap tomorrow. A merry song, come: it grows late, we will to bed. Thou wilt forget me, when I am gone.
Doll. By my troth thou'lt set me a weeping, if thou sayest so: prove that I ever dress myself handsome till thy return. Well, hearken the end.

Painted by HENRY FUSELI, R.A.
Engraved by WILLIAM LENEY.

Ph. XLVIII.* 191.*

KING
HENRY IV.
PART II.

(1)

XLIX.

THE SECOND PART OF

KING HENRY THE FOURTH.

Act III. Scene 2.

JUSTICE SHALLOW'S SEAT IN GLOUCESTERSHIRE.

Shallow, Silence, Falstaff, Bardolph, Boy, Mouldy, Shadow, Wart, Feeble, and Bull-calf.

Fal. ———O, give me the spare men, and spare me the great ones. Put me a caliver into Wart's hand, Bardolph.

Bard. Hold, Wart, traverse; thus, thus, thus.

Fal. Come, manage me your caliver. So:—very well:—go to:—very good:—exceeding good.—O, give me always a little, lean, old, chapped, bald shot.—Well said, Wart; thou 'rt a good scab: hold, there 's a tester for thee.

Painted by James Durno.
Engraved by Thomas Ryder.

Pl. XIV.

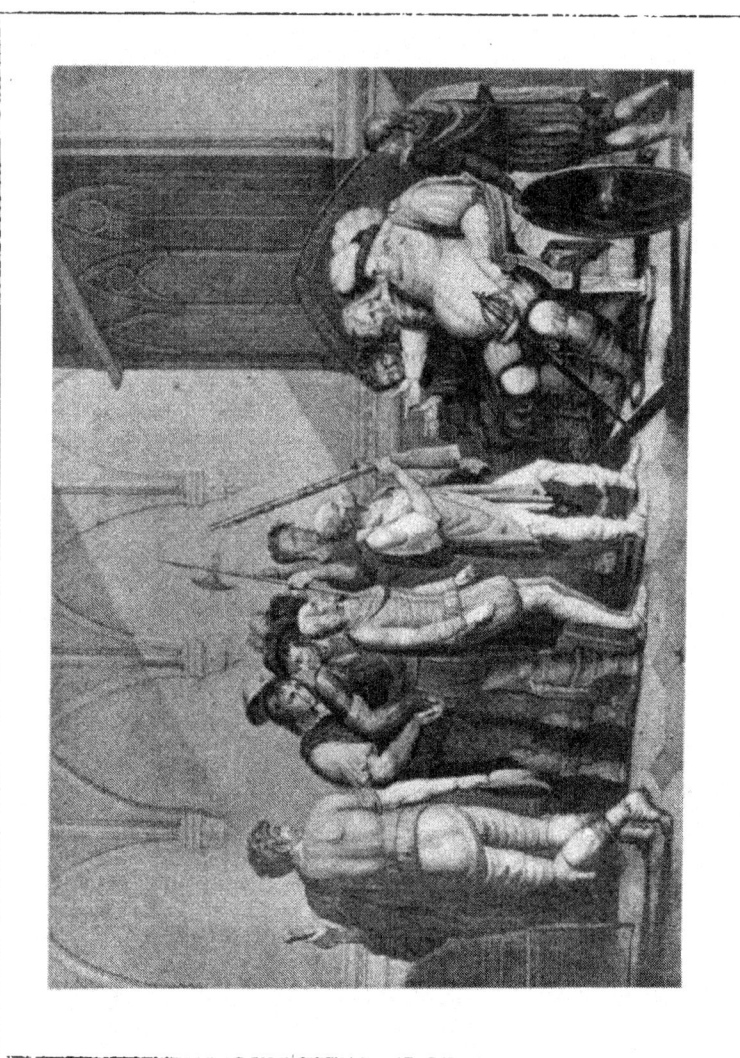

KING
HENRY IV.
PART II.

(2)

L.

THE SECOND PART OF
KING HENRY THE FOURTH.

Act IV. Scene 4.

THE PALACE AT WESTMINSTER.

King Henry asleep; Prince of Wales.

P. Hen. —————— My gracious lord! my father!
This sleep is sound indeed; this is a sleep,
That from this golden rigol hath divorc'd
So many English kings. Thy due, from me,
Is tears, and heavy sorrows of the blood;
Which nature, love, and filial tenderness,
Shall, O dear father, pay thee plenteously:
My due, from thee, is this imperial crown;
Which, as immediate from thy place and blood,
Derives itself to me. Lo, here it sits,—
                                [*Putting it on his head.*
Which Heaven shall guard; And put the world's whole strength
Into one giant arm, it shall not force
This lineal honour from me: This from thee
Will I to mine leave, as 't is left to me.

Painted by JOSIAH BOYDELL.
Engraved by ROBERT THEW.

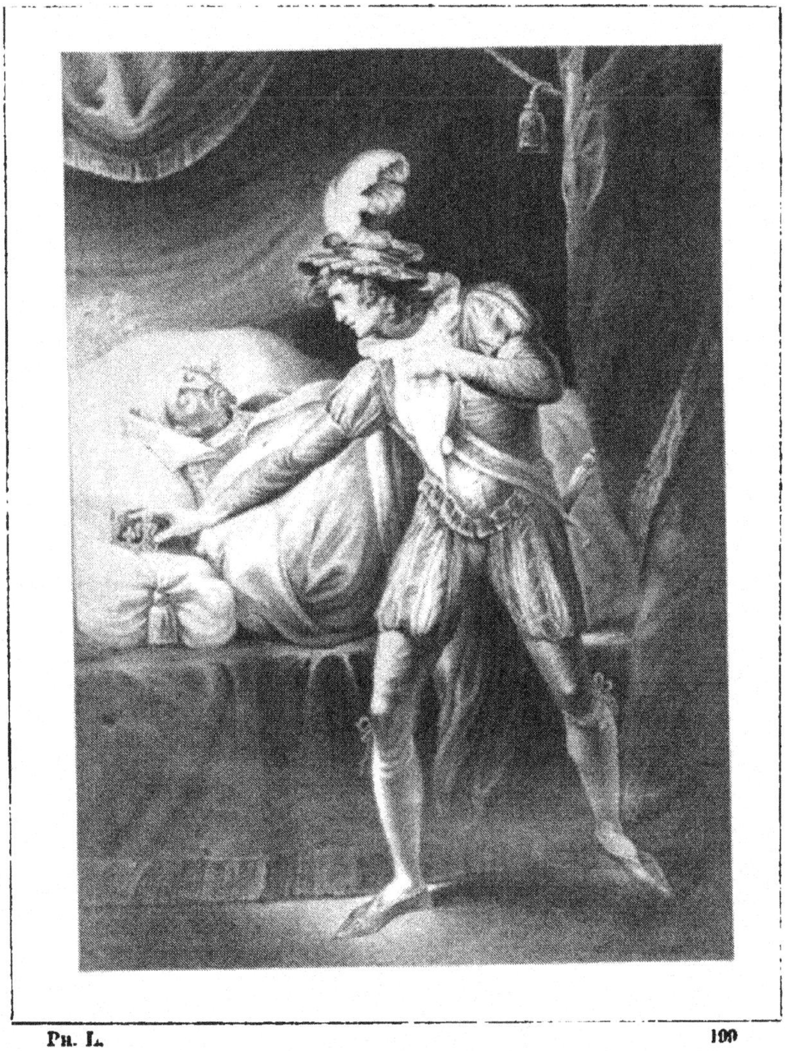

Pt. I. 190

KING HENRY IV, PART II.

LI.

THE SECOND PART OF
KING HENRY THE FOURTH.

Act IV. Scene 4.

THE PALACE AT WESTMINSTER.

King Henry, and the Prince of Wales.

P. Hen. ————There is your crown:
And He that wears the crown immortally,
Long guard it yours! If I affect it more,
Than as your honour, and as your renown,
Let me no more from this obedience rise,—
(Which my most true and inward duteous spirit
Teacheth)—this prostrate and exterior bending!
Heaven witness with me, when I here came in
And found no course of breath within your majesty,
How cold it struck my heart! If I do feign,
O, let me in my present wildness die;
And never live to show th' incredulous world
The noble change that I have purposed!

Painted by JOSIAH BOYDELL.
Engraved by ROBERT THEW.

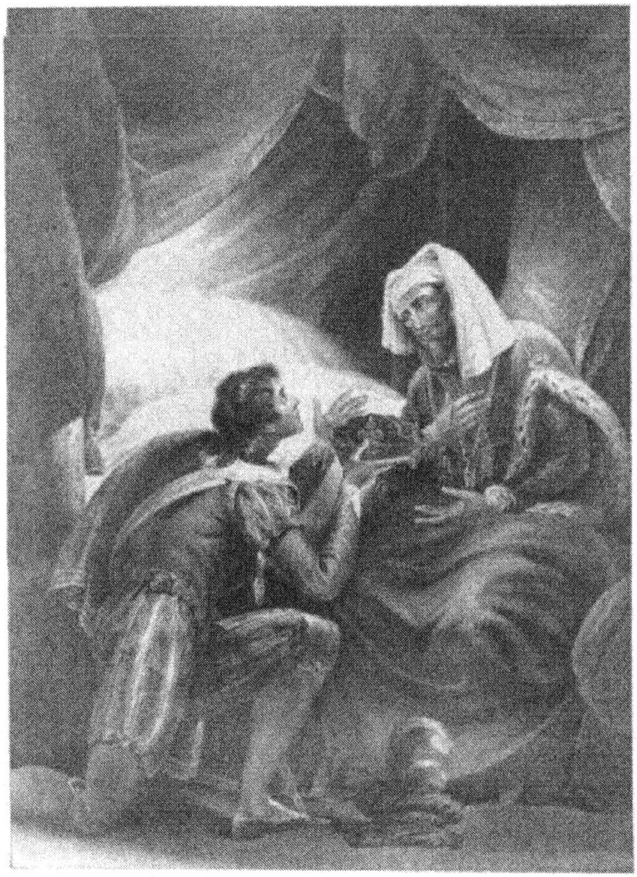

Pl. LI.

KING HENRY V.

LII.

KING HENRY THE FIFTH.

Act II. Scene 2.

SOUTHAMPTON.

Exeter, Bedford, and Westmoreland; the King, Scroop, Cambridge, Grey, and Attendants.

   K. Hen. ———— Why, how now, gentlemen ?
What see you in those papers, that you lose
So much complexion ?—look ye, how they change !
Their cheeks are paper.—Why, what read you there,
That hath so cowarded and chas'd your blood
Out of appearance ?
   Cam.   I do confess my fault ;
And do submit me to your highness' mercy.
   Grey. Scroop. To which we all appeal.

Painted by Henry Fuseli, R.A.
Engraved by Robert Thew.

Pl. LII.

KING HENRY VI.
PART I.

LIII.

THE FIRST PART OF
KING HENRY THE SIXTH.

Act II. Scene 3.

THE COUNTESS OF AUVERGNE'S CASTLE.

The Countess, Porter, Talbot, &c.

Count. This is a riddling merchant for the nonce;
He will be here, and yet he is not here:
How can these contrarieties agree?
Tal. That will I show you presently.
          [*He winds a horn. Drums heard; then a
            Peal of Ordnance. The Gates being
            forced, enter Soldiers.*
How say you, madam? are you now persuaded
That Talbot is but shadow of himself?
These are his substance, sinews, arms, and strength,
With which he yoketh your rebellious necks;
Razeth your cities, and subverts your towns,
And in a moment makes them desolate.

Painted by JOHN OPIE, R.A.
Engraved by ROBERT THEW.

Ph. LIII.

KING
HENRY VI.
PART I.

(2)

LIV.

THE FIRST PART OF
KING HENRY THE SIXTH.

Act II. Scene 4.

LONDON; THE TEMPLE GARDEN.

Earls of Somerset, Suffolk, and Warwick; Richard Plantagenet, Vernon, and another Lawyer.

   Plan. Since you are tongue-tied, and so loth to speak,
In dumb significants proclaim your thoughts:
Let him that is a true-born gentleman,
And stands upon the honour of his birth,
If he suppose that I have pleaded truth,
From off this brier pluck a white rose with me.
   Som. Let him that is no coward, nor no flatterer,
But dare maintain the party of the truth,
Pluck a red rose from off this thorn with me.

Painted by JOSIAH BOYDELL.
Engraved by JOHN OGBORNE.

Pl. LIV.

KING HENRY VI.
PART I.

LV.

THE FIRST PART OF

KING HENRY THE SIXTH.

Act II. Scene 5.

A ROOM IN THE TOWER.

Mortimer in a chair, Jailor, and Richard Plantagenet.

Jailor. My lord, your loving nephew now is come.
Mor. Richard Plantagenet, my friend ?   Is he come ?
Plan. Ay, noble uncle, thus ignobly us'd,
Your nephew, late-despised Richard, comes.
 Mor. Direct mine arms, I may embrace his neck,
And in his bosom spend my latter gasp :
O, tell me, when my lips do touch his cheeks,
That I may kindly give one fainting kiss.—

Painted by JAMES NORTHCOTE, R.A.
Engraved by ROBERT THEW.

Ph. LV. 219

KING
HENRY VI.
PART II.

LVI.

THE SECOND PART OF
KING HENRY THE SIXTH.

Act I. Scene 4.

LONDON; THE DUKE OF GLOSTER'S GARDEN.

Mother Jourdain, Hume, Southwell, Bolingbroke, and the Duchess.

Bol. Madam, sit you, and fear not; whom we raise,
We will make fast within a hallow'd verge.
 [*Here they perform the ceremonies appertaining,
 and make the circle; Bolingbroke, or South-
 well, reads,* Conjuro te, &c. *It thunders and
 lightens terribly; then the Spirit riseth.*
Spir. Adsum.
M. Jourd. Asmath,
By the eternal God, whose name and power
Thou tremblest at, answer that I shall ask;
For till thou speak thou shalt not pass from hence.

Painted by JOHN OPIE, R.A.
Engraved by C. G. PLAYTER *and* R. THEW.

Pl. LVI.

KING
HENRY VI.
PART II.

(2)

LVII.

THE SECOND PART OF

KING HENRY THE SIXTH.

Act III. Scene 3.

CARDINAL BEAUFORT'S BEDCHAMBER.

King Henry, Salisbury, and Warwick. The Cardinal in bed.

 K. Hen. O thou eternal Mover of the heavens,
Look with a gentle eye upon this wretch!
O, beat away the busy meddling fiend
That lays strong siege unto this wretch's soul,
And from his bosom purge this black despair!
 War. See, how the pangs of death do make him grin.
 Sal. Disturb him not, let him pass peaceably.
 K. Hen. Peace to his soul, if God's good pleasure be!
Lord cardinal, if thou think'st on heaven's bliss,
Hold up thy hand, make signal of thy hope.—
He dies, and makes no sign; O God, forgive him!

Painted by Sir Joshua Reynolds.
Engraved by Caroline Watson.

Fig. LVII.

KING
HENRY VI.
PART III.

LVIII.

THE THIRD PART OF
KING HENRY THE SIXTH.

Act I. Scene 3.

A FIELD OF BATTLE BETWEEN SANDAL CASTLE AND WAKEFIELD.

Rutland and his Tutor, Clifford and Soldiers.

Clif. Chaplain, away! thy priesthood saves thy life.
As for the brat of this accursed duke,
Whose father slew my father, he shall die.
   Tut. And I, my lord, will bear him company.
   Clif. Soldiers, away with him.
   Tut. Ah, Clifford! murther not this innocent child,
Lest thou be hated both of God and man.
                             [*Exit, forced off by Soldiers.*
   Clif. How now! is he dead already? Or is it fear
That makes him close his eyes?—I'll open them.

Painted by JAMES NORTHCOTE, R.A.
Engraved by C. G. PLAYTER *and* T. RYDER.

Pn. LVIII.

THE NEW YORK
PUBLIC LIBRARY

ASTOR, LENOX
TILDEN FOUNDA

KING HENRY VI.
PART III.

(2)

LIX.

THE THIRD PART OF
KING HENRY THE SIXTH.

Act II. Scene 5.

A FIELD OF BATTLE, NEAR TOWTON, IN YORKSHIRE.

King Henry. Son that has killed his Father—Father that has killed his Son.

Fath. Thou that so stoutly hast resisted me,
Give me thy gold, if thou hast any gold;
For I have bought it with an hundred blows.
But let me see:—is this our foeman's face?
Ah, no, no, no, it is mine only son!
Ah, boy, if any life be left in thee,
Throw up thine eye; see, see, what showers arise,
Blown with the windy tempest of my heart,
Upon thy wounds, that kill mine eye and heart!
O, pity, God, this miserable age!
What stratagems, how fell, how butcherly,
Erroneous, mutinous, and unnatural,
This deadly quarrel daily doth beget!
O boy, thy father gave thee life too soon,
And hath bereft thee of thy life too late!

Painted by JOSIAH BOYDELL.
Engraved by JOHN OGBORNE.

PH. LIX.

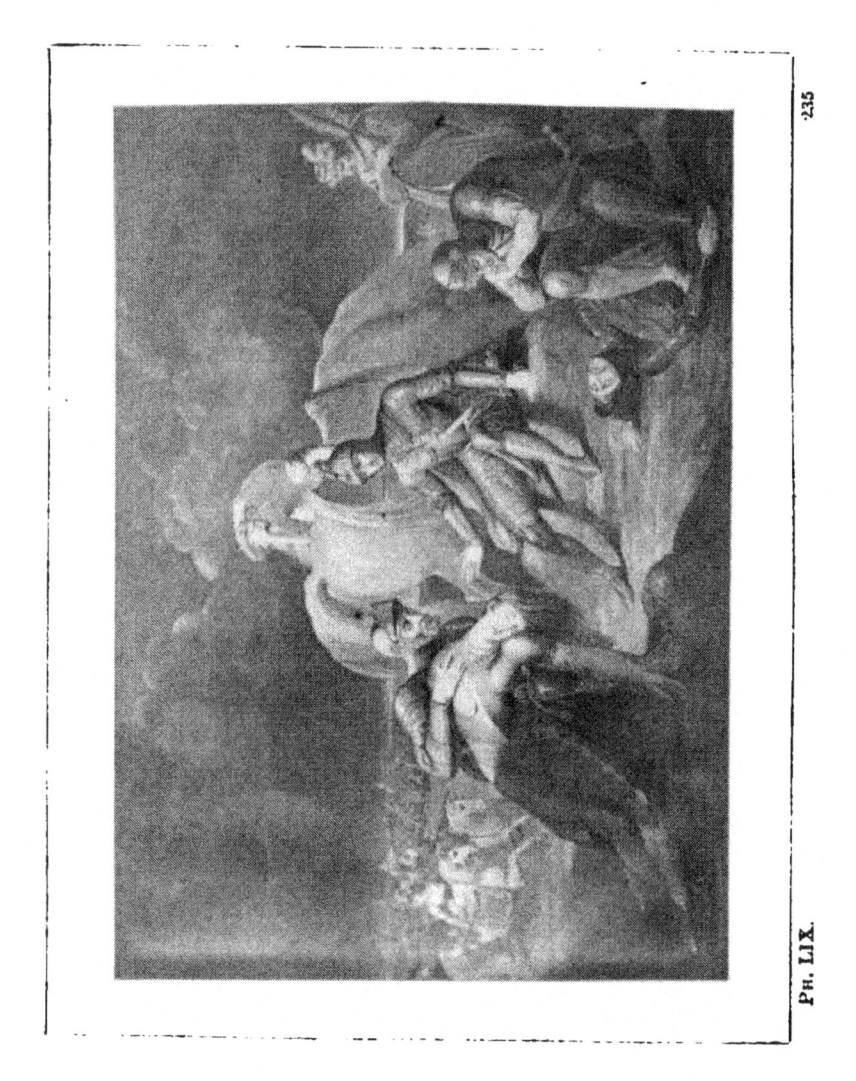

KING HENRY VI.
PART III.

LX.

THE THIRD PART OF

KING HENRY THE SIXTH.

Act IV. Scene 5.

A PARK, NEAR MIDDLEHAM CASTLE, IN YORKSHIRE.

*King Edward and Huntsman; Gloster, Hastings, and
Sir William Stanley in the distance.*

Hunt. This way, my lord; for this way lies the game.
K. Edw. Nay, this way, man; see where the huntsmen stand.
Now, brother of Gloster, lord Hastings, and the rest,
Stand you thus close to steal the bishop's deer?

    *   *   *   *   *

K. Edw. Huntsman, what say'st thou? wilt thou go along?
Hunt. Better do so than tarry and be hang'd.
Glo. Come then, away; let 's have no more ado.
K. Edw. Bishop, farewell: shield thee from Warwick's frown;
And pray that I may repossess the crown.

Painted by WILLIAM MILLER.
Engraved by JOHN BAPTIST MICHEL *and* WILLIAM LENEY.

Pn. LX.

KING
HENRY VI.
PART III.

LXI.

THE THIRD PART OF

KING HENRY THE SIXTH.

Act V. Scene 7.

THE PALACE IN LONDON.

King Edward, the Queen, with the young Prince, Clarence, Gloster, Hastings, and Attendants.

K. Edw. Come hither, Bess, and let me kiss my boy:
Young Ned, for thee, thine uncles and myself
Have in our armours watch'd the winter's night;
Went all afoot in summer's scalding heat,
That thou might'st repossess the crown in peace;
And of our labours thou shalt reap the gain.
  Glo. I 'll blast his harvest, if your head were laid;
For yet I am not look'd on in the world.
This shoulder was ordain'd so thick to heave;
And heave it shall some weight, or break my back:
Work thou the way, and thou shalt execute.
                              [*Aside.*

Painted by JAMES NORTHCOTE, R.A.
Engraved by JOHN BAPTIST MICHEL.

Ph. LXI.   243

KING RICHARD III.

(1)

LXII.

KING RICHARD THE THIRD.

Act III. Scene 1.

LONDON.

The Prince of Wales, the Duke of York, his brother, Dukes of Gloster and Buckingham, Cardinal Bourchier, Lord Hastings, the Lord Mayor, and his Train.

Buck. Now, in good time, here comes the duke of York.
Prince. Richard of York! how fares our noble brother?
York. Well, my dread lord; so must I call you now.
Prince. Ay, brother; to our grief, as it is yours:
Too late he died, that might have kept that title,
Which by his death hath lost much majesty.

Painted by JAMES NORTHCOTE, R.A.
Engraved by ROBERT THEW.

Pl. LXII.

KING
RICHARD III.
—
(2)

LXIII.

KING RICHARD THE THIRD.

Act IV. Scene 3.

LONDON; THE TOWER.

The Murder of the Princes, as described by Tyrrel.

Tyr. Dighton and Forrest, whom I did suborn
To do this piece of ruthless butchery,
Albeit they were flesh'd villains, bloody dogs,
Melting with tenderness and mild compassion,
Wept like to children, in their death's sad story.
"O thus," quoth Dighton, "lay the gentle babes,"—
"Thus, thus," quoth Forrest, "girdling one another
Within their alabaster innocent arms:
Their lips were four red roses on a stalk,
And, in their summer beauty, kiss'd each other.
A book of prayers on their pillow lay:
Which once," quoth Forrest, "almost chang'd my mind;
But, O, the devil"—there the villain stopp'd;
When Dighton thus told on,—" we smothered
The most replenished sweet work of Nature,
That, from the prime creation, e'er she fram'd!"

Painted by JAMES NORTHCOTE, R.A.
Engraved by FRANCIS LEGAT.

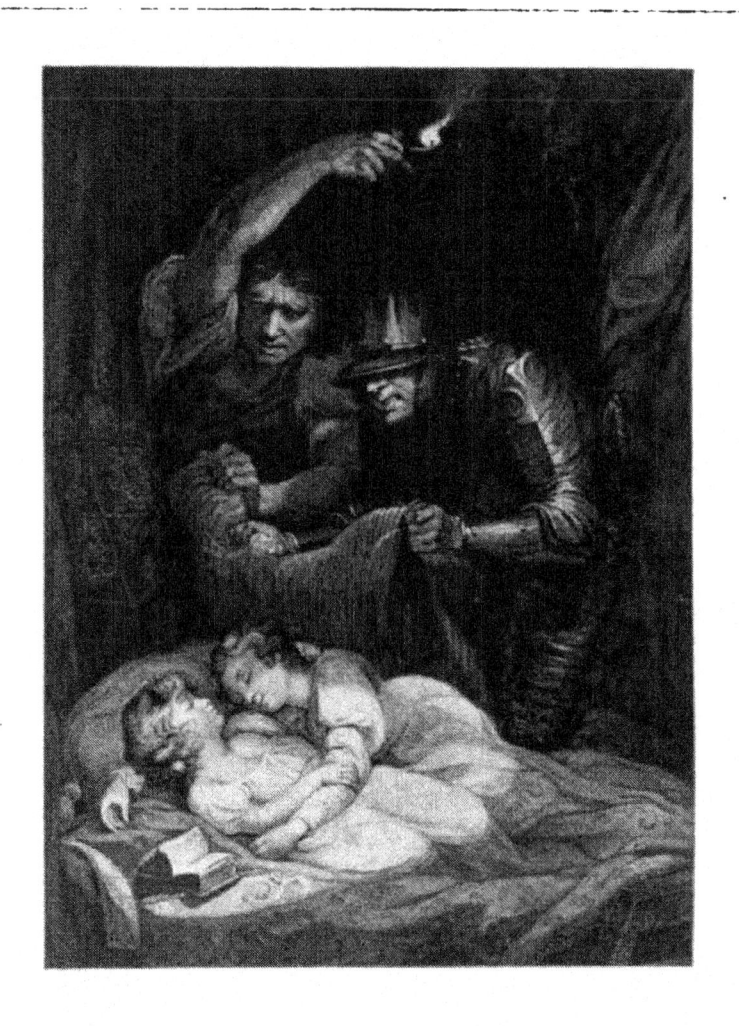

Ph. LXIII.

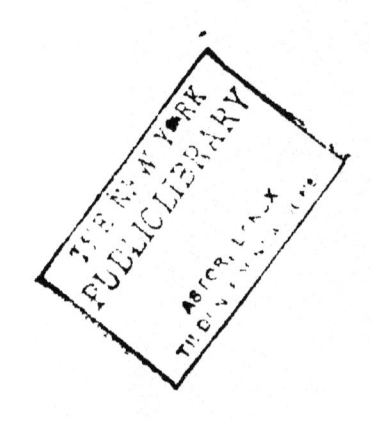

KING RICHARD III.

LXIV.

KING RICHARD THE THIRD.

Act IV. Scene 3.

LONDON ; THE TOWER.

The Burying of the Princes, as described by Tyrrel.

   K. Rich. Kind Tyrrel! am I happy in thy news?
   Tyr. If to have done the thing you gave in charge
Beget your happiness, be happy then,
For it is done.
   K. Rich.   But didst thou see them dead?
   Tyr. I did, my lord.
   K. Rich.   And buried, gentle Tyrrel?
   Tyr. The chaplain of the Tower hath buried them;
But where to say the truth, I do not know.

Painted by JAMES NORTHCOTE, R.A.
Engraved by WILLIAM SKELTON.

Pu. LXIV.

KING
HENRY VIII.

(1)

LXV.

KING HENRY THE EIGHTH.

Act I. Scene 4.

YORK PLACE.

---

*Cardinal Wolsey, Lord Sands, Anne Bullen,
King Henry, &c.*

K. Hen. My lord chamberlain,
Prithee, come hither: What fair lady 's that?
    Cham. An 't please your grace, sir Thomas Bullen's
        daughter,
The viscount Rochford, one of her highness' women.
    K. Hen. By Heaven, she is a dainty one.—Sweetheart,
I were unmannerly to take you out,
And not to kiss you.—

Painted by Thomas Stothard, R.A.
Engraved by Isaac Taylor.

Pl. LXV.

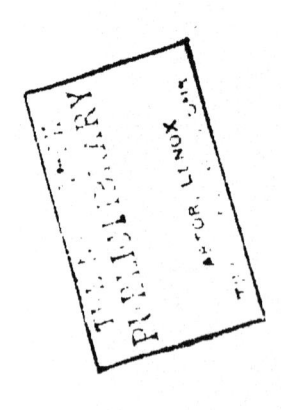

KING
HENRY VIII.
—
(2)

LXVI.

KING HENRY THE EIGHTH.

Act III. Scene 1.

THE PALACE AT BRIDEWELL; THE QUEEN'S APARTMENTS.

The Queen and her Women at work; Cardinals Wolsey and Campeius.

    Wol. May it please you, noble madam, to withdraw
Into your private chamber, we shall give you
The full cause of our coming.
    Q. Kath.   Speak it here;
There's nothing I have done yet, o' my conscience,
Deserves a corner: 'Would all other women
Could speak this with as free a soul as I do!
My lords, I care not, (so much I am happy
Above a number,) if my actions
Were tried by every tongue, every eye saw them,
Envy and base opinion set against them,
I know my life so even: If your business
Seek me out, and that way I am wife in,
Out with it boldly: Truth loves open dealing.

Painted by the Rev. WILLIAM PETERS, R.A.
Engraved by ROBERT THEW.

Pl. LXVI.

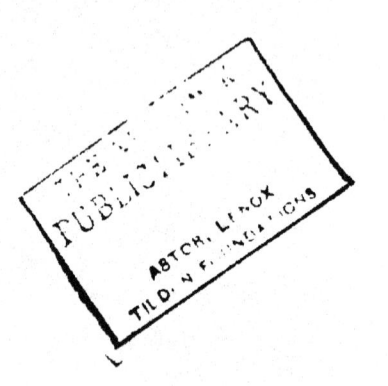

KING
HENRY VIII.

(3)

LXVII.

KING HENRY THE EIGHTH.

Act IV. Scene 2.

THE ABBEY OF LEICESTER.

The Abbot of Leicester, Wolsey, Northumberland, and Attendants.

(THE RECEPTION OF THE CARDINAL, AS DESCRIBED BY GRIFFITH TO QUEEN KATHARINE.)

Grif. At last, with easy roads, he came to Leicester,
Lodg'd in the abbey; where the reverend abbot,
With all his convent, honourably receiv'd him;
To whom he gave these words,—"O father abbot,
An old man, broken with the storms of state,
Is come to lay his weary bones among ye;
Give him a little earth for charity!"
So went to bed: where eagerly his sickness
Pursued him still; and, three nights after this,
About the hour of eight, (which he himself
Foretold should be his last,) full of repentance,
Continual meditations, tears, and sorrows,
He gave his honours to the world again,
His blessed part to Heaven, and slept in peace.

Painted by RICHARD WESTALL, R.A.
Engraved by ROBERT THEW.

PH. LXVII.

KING
HENRY VIII.

(4)

LXVIII.

KING HENRY THE EIGHTH.

Act V. Scene 4.

THE PALACE.

The Christening of the Princess Elizabeth.

 Cran.   Let me speak, sir,
For Heaven now bids me; and the words I utter
Let none think flattery, for they 'll find them truth.
This royal infant, (Heaven still move about her!)
Though in her cradle, yet now promises
Upon this land a thousand thousand blessings,
Which time shall bring to ripeness: She shall be
(But few now living can behold that goodness)
A pattern to all princes living with her,
And all that shall succeed.—

Painted by the Rev. WILLIAM PETERS, R.A.
Engraved by JOSEPH COLLYER.

Pl. LXVIII.

TROILUS
AND
CRESSIDA.

(1)

LXIX.

TROILUS AND CRESSIDA.

Act II. Scene 2.

TROY.

Priam, Hector, Troilus, Paris, Helenus. Enter Cassandra, raving.

 Cas. Cry, Trojans, cry! lend me ten thousand eyes,
And I will fill them with prophetic tears.
 Hect. Peace, sister, peace.
 Cas. Virgins and boys, mid-age, and wrinkled old,
Soft infancy, that nothing canst but cry,
Add to my clamours! let us pay betimes
A moiety of that mass of moan to come.
Cry, Trojans, cry! practise your eyes with tears!
Troy must not be, nor goodly Ilion stand;
Our firebrand brother, Paris, burns us all.
Cry, Trojans, cry! a Helen, and a woe:
Cry, cry! Troy burns, or else let Helen go.

Painted by GEORGE ROMNEY.
Engraved by FRANCIS LEGAT.

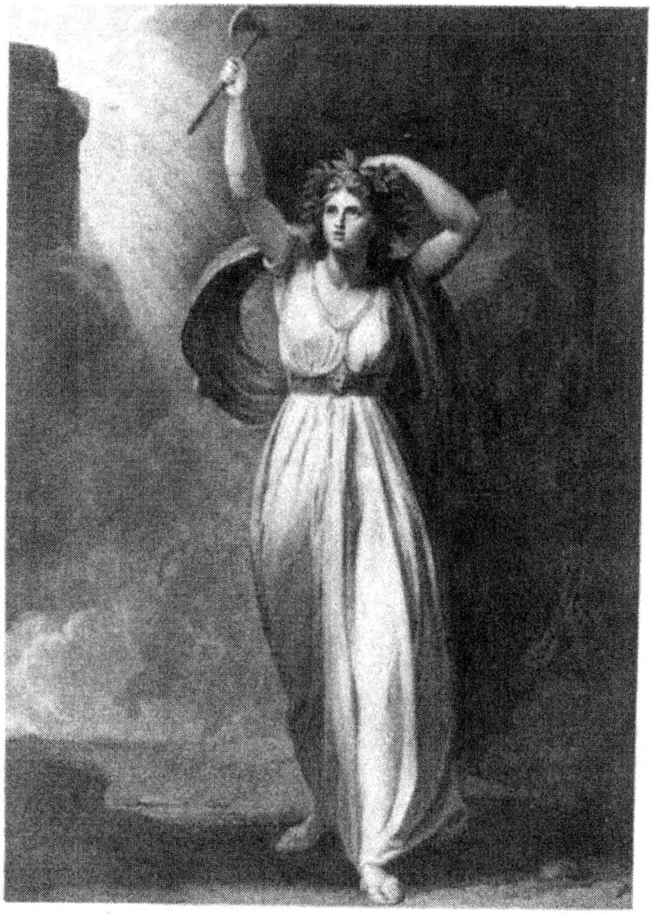

Pr. LXIX.

THE NEW YORK
PUBLIC LIBRARY

ASTOR, LENOX
TILDEN FOUNDATIONS

TROILUS AND CRESSIDA.

LXX.

TROILUS AND CRESSIDA.

Act V. Scene 2.

CALCHAS' TENT.

Diomedes and Cressida. Troilus, Ulysses, and Thersites, at a distance.

  Dio.   And so, good night.
  Cres. Nay, but you part in anger.
  Tro.   Doth that grieve thee?
O wither'd truth!
  Ulyss.   Why, how now, lord?
  Tro.   By Jove,
I will be patient.
  Cres.   Guardian!—why, Greek!
  Dio. Pho, Pho! adieu; you palter.
  Cres. In faith, I do not; come hither once again.
  Ulyss. You shake, my lord, at something; will you go?
You will break out.
  Tro.   She strokes his cheek!
  Ulyss.   Come, come.

Painted by ANGELICA KAUFFMAN, R.A.
Engraved by LUIGI SCHIAVONETTI.

Pl. LXX.

CORIOLANUS.

(1)

LXXI.

CORIOLANUS.

Act II. Scene 1.

(BASSO-RELIEVO.)

ROME.

Coriolanus, Menenius, Cominius, Volumnia, Virgilia, &c.

 Com.   Look, sir, your mother!
 Cor. O! you have, I know, petition'd all the gods
For my prosperity.   [*Kneels.*
 Vol.   Nay, my good soldier, up!
My gentle Marcius, worthy Caius,
And by deed-achieving honour newly nam'd,
What is it? Coriolanus must I call thee?
But, O thy wife!
 Cor.   My gracious silence, hail!
Wouldst thou have laugh'd had I come coffin'd home,
That weep'st to see me triumph? Ah, my dear,
Such eyes the widows in Corioli wear,
And mothers that lack sons.

 Modelled by The Hon. ANNE SEYMOUR DAMER.
 Engraved by WILLIAM LENEY.

Pl. LXXI.

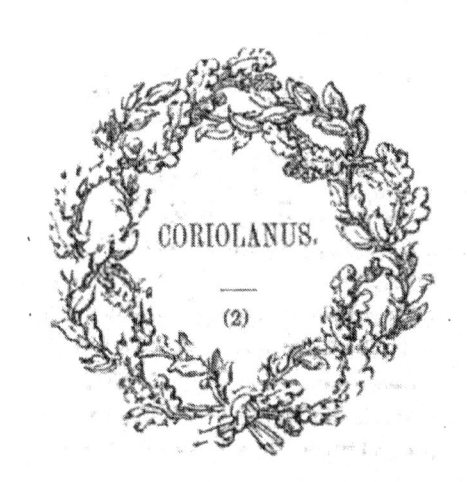

CORIOLANUS.

(2)

LXXII.

CORIOLANUS.

Act V. Scene 3.

THE TENT OF CORIOLANUS.

Coriolanus, Aufidius, Virgilia, Volumnia, young Marcius, Valeria, and Attendants.

   Vol.   Say, my request 's unjust,
And spurn me back: But, if it be not so,
Thou art not honest; and the gods will plague thee,
That thou restrain'st from me the duty which
To a mother's part belongs.—He turns away:
Down, ladies! let us shame him with our knees.
To his surname Coriolanus 'longs more pride
Than pity to our prayers. Down: An end:
This is the last:—So we will home to Rome,
And die among our neighbours.—Nay, behold us:
This boy, that cannot tell what he would have,
But kneels, and holds up hands, for fellowship,
Does reason our petition with more strength
Than thou hast to deny 't.—Come, let us go.

Painted by GAVIN HAMILTON.

Engraved by JAMES CALDWALL.

Pl. LXXII.

TITUS ANDRONICUS

P P

LXXIII.

TITUS ANDRONICUS.

Act IV. Scene 1.

TITUS'S HOUSE.

Titus and Marcus. Young Lucius pursued by Lavinia.

Boy. Help, grandsire, help! my aunt Lavinia
Follows me everywhere, I know not why.
Good uncle Marcus, see how swift she comes!
Alas, sweet aunt, I know not what you mean.

Painted and Engraved by Thomas Kirk.

Pb. LXXIII.

THE NEW YORK
PUBLIC LIBRARY
ASTOR, LENOX
TILDEN FOUNDATIONS

ROMEO
AND
JULIET.

(1)

LXXIV.

ROMEO AND JULIET.

Act I. Scene 5.

A HALL IN CAPULET'S HOUSE.

———

Romeo, Juliet, Nurse, &c., with the Guests and the Maskers.

Rom. If I profane with my unworthiest hand
                              [*To Juliet.*
    This holy shrine, the gentle sin is this,—
My lips, two blushing pilgrims, ready stand
    To smooth that rough touch with a tender kiss.
Jul. Good pilgrim, you do wrong your hand too much,
    Which mannerly devotion shows in this ;
For saints have hands that pilgrims' hands do touch,
    And palm to palm is holy palmers' kiss.

———

Painted by WILLIAM MILLER.

Engraved by GEORGE SIGMUND *and* JOHN GOTTLIEB FACIUS.

Pl. LXXIV.

ROMEO AND JULIET.

(2)

LXXV.

ROMEO AND JULIET.

Act IV. Scene 5.

JULIET'S CHAMBER; JULIET ON THE BED.

Friar Laurence, Capulet, Lady Capulet, Paris, Friar, Nurse, Musicians, &c.

    Cap. Despis'd, distressed, hated, martyr'd, kill'd!—
Uncomfortable time! why cam'st thou now
To murther, murther, our solemnity?—
O child! O child!—my soul, and not my child!—
Dead art thou!—alack! my child is dead!
And, with my child, my joys are buried!
    Fri. Peace, ho, for shame! confusion's cure lives not
In these confusions. Heaven and yourself
Had part in this fair maid; now Heaven hath all,
And all the better is it for the maid:
Your part in her you could not keep from death;
But Heaven keeps his part in eternal life.

Painted by JOHN OPIE, R.A.

Engraved by GEORGE SIGMUND *and* JOHN GOTTLIEB FACIUS.

Pl. LXXV.

ROMEO
AND
JULIET.

(3)

LXXVI.

ROMEO AND JULIET.

Act V. Scene 3.

A MONUMENT BELONGING TO THE CAPULETS.

Romeo and Paris dead; Juliet, and Friar Laurence.

 Fri.   Romeo!— [*Advances.*
Alack, alack, what blood is this, which stains
The stony entrance of this sepulchre?—
What mean these masterless and gory swords
To lie discolour'd by this place of peace?
          [*Enters the Monument.*
Romeo! O, pale!—Who else? what, Paris too?
And steep'd in blood?—Ah, what an unkind hour
Is guilty of this lamentable chance!—
The lady stirs.   [*Juliet wakes.*
 Jul. O, comfortable friar! where is my lord?
I do remember well where I should be,
And there I am: Where is my Romeo?

Painted by JAMES NORTHCOTE, R.A.
Engraved by PETER SIMON.

PH. LXXVI.

TIMON OF ATHENS.

LXXVII.

TIMON OF ATHENS.

Act IV. Scene 3.

A WOOD.

Timon, Alcibiades, Phrynia, and Timandra.

Alcib. When I have laid proud Athens on a heap,—
Tim. Warr'st thou 'gainst Athens?
Alcib.   Ay, Timon, and have cause.
Tim. The gods confound them all in thy conquest; and thee after, when thou hast conquer'd!
Alcib. Why me, Timon?
Tim. That, by killing of villains, thou wast born to conquer my country.
Put up thy gold: Go on,—here's gold,—go on;
Be as a planetary plague, when Jove
Will o'er some high-vic'd city hang his poison
In the sick air: Let not thy sword skip one:
Pity not honour'd age for his white beard,
He's an usurer: Strike me the counterfeit matron;
It is her habit only that is honest.

Painted by JOHN OPIE, R.A.
Engraved by ROBERT THEW.

Pl. LXXVII.

JULIUS CÆSAR.

LXXVIII.

JULIUS CÆSAR.

Act IV. Scene 3.

BRUTUS'S TENT, IN THE CAMP NEAR SARDIS.

Brutus and the Ghost of Cæsar.

Bru. Let me see, let me see:—Is not the leaf turn'd down
Where I left reading? Here it is, I think.
          [He sits down.
   Enter the Ghost.
How ill this taper burns!—Ha! who comes here?
I think it is the weakness of mine eyes
That shapes this monstrous apparition.
It comes upon me:—Art thou anything?
Art thou some god, some angel, or some devil,
That mak'st my blood cold, and my hair to stare?
Speak to me what thou art.
 Ghost. Thy evil spirit, Brutus.
 Bru.   Why com'st thou?
 Ghost. To tell thee, thou shalt see me at Philippi.
 Bru. Well: Then I shall see thee again?
 Ghost.   Ay, at Philippi.
          [Ghost vanishes.

Painted by RICHARD WESTALL, R.A.

Engraved by EDWARD SCRIVEN.

Pu. LXXVIII.   311

MACBETH.

(1)

LXXIX.

MACBETH.

Act I. Scene 3.

A HEATH.

Macbeth, Banquo, and the three Witches.

1 *Witch.* Banquo, and Macbeth, all hail!
Macb. Stay, you imperfect speakers, tell me more:
By Sinel's death, I know I am thane of Glamis;
But how of Cawdor? the thane of Cawdor lives,
A prosperous gentleman; and, to be king,
Stands not within the prospect of belief,
No more than to be Cawdor. Say, from whence
You owe this strange intelligence? or why
Upon this blasted heath you stop our way
With such prophetic greeting?—Speak, I charge you.
                    [*Witches vanish.*
Ban. The earth hath bubbles, as the water has,
And these are of them: Whither are they vanish'd?
Macb. Into the air: and what seem'd corporal, melted
As breath into the wind.—'Would they had staid!

Painted by HENRY FUSELI, R.A.
Engraved by JAMES CALDWALL.

PL. LXXIX.

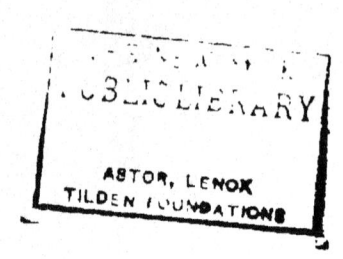

MACBETH.

(2)

LXXX.

MACBETH.

Act I. Scene 5.

INVERNESS; A ROOM IN MACBETH'S CASTLE.

Lady Macbeth, a letter in her hand.

Lady M.   The raven himself is hoarse
That croaks the fatal entrance of Duncan
Under my battlements. Come, you spirits
That tend on mortal thoughts, unsex me here;
And fill me, from the crown to the toe, top-full
Of direst cruelty! make thick my blood,
Stop up the access and passage to remorse;
That no compunctious visitings of nature
Shake my fell purpose, nor keep peace between
The effect, and it! Come to my woman's breasts,
And take my milk for gall, you murthering ministers,
Wherever in your sightless substances
You wait on nature's mischief! Come, thick night,
And pall thee in the dunnest smoke of hell!
That my keen knife see not the wound it makes;
Nor heaven peep through the blanket of the dark,
To cry, " Hold, Hold!"—Great Glamis, worthy Cawdor!

Painted by RICHARD WESTALL, R.A.
Engraved by JAMES PARKER.

Ph. LXXX.   319

MACBETH.

(3)

LXXXI.

MACBETH.

Act IV. Scene 1.

A DARK CAVE, IN THE MIDDLE A CAULDRON BOILING.

Three Witches, Macbeth, Hecate, &c.

1 *Witch.* Show!   2 *Witch.* Show!   3 *Witch.* Show!
All. Show his eyes, and grieve his heart;
Come like shadows, so depart.

Eight Kings appear, and pass over the Stage in order; the last with a Glass in his hand; Banquo following.

  Macb. Thou art too like the spirit of Banquo; down!
Thy crown does sear mine eyeballs:—And thy hair,
Thou other gold-bound brow, is like the first:—
A third is like the former:—Filthy hags!
Why do you show me this?—A fourth?—Start, eyes!
What! will the line stretch out to the crack of doom?
Another yet?—A seventh?—I'll see no more:—
And yet the eighth appears, who bears a glass
Which shows me many more; and some I see,
That two-fold balls and treble sceptres carry:
Horrible sight!—Now, I see, 't is true;
For the blood-bolter'd Banquo smiles upon me,
And points at them for his.—

Painted by Sir Joshua Reynolds, R.A.

Engraved by Robert Thew.

Рис. LXXXI.

HAMLET.

(1)

LXXXII.

HAMLET.

Act I. Scene 4.

A PLATFORM BEFORE THE CASTLE OF ELSINEUR.

Hamlet, Horatio, Marcellus, and the Ghost.

Ham. It wafts me still:—Go on, I'll follow thee.
Mar. You shall not go, my lord.
Ham.   Hold off your hand.
Hor. Be rul'd, you shall not go.
Ham.   My fate cries out,
And makes each petty artery in this body
As hardy as the Nemean lion's nerve.—
                               [*Ghost beckons.*
Still am I call'd;—unhand me, gentlemen;
                          [*Breaking from them.*
By heaven, I'll make a ghost of him that lets me:
I say, away:—Go on, I'll follow thee.

Painted by HENRY FUSELI, R.A.

Engraved by ROBERT THEW.

PH. LXXXII.

HAMLET.

(2)

LXXXIII.

HAMLET.

Act IV. Scene 5.

ELSINEUR; A ROOM IN THE CASTLE.

King, Queen, Laertes, Ophelia, &c.

Oph. There's fennel for you, and columbines:—there's rue for you; and here's some for me:—we may call it herb-grace o' Sundays:—oh, you must wear your rue with a difference.—There's a daisy:—I would give you some violets; but they withered all, when my father died:—They say, he made a good end,—

For bonny sweet Robin is all my joy,—

Laer. Thought and affliction, passion, hell itself,
She turns to favour, and to prettiness.

Oph. And will he not come again?
And will he not come again?
No, no, he is dead,
Go to thy death-bed,
He never will come again.

His beard as white as snow,
All flaxen was his poll:
He is gone, he is gone,
And we cast away moan:
Gramercy on his soul!

And of all christian souls! I pray God. God be wi' you!
Laer. Do you see this, O God? [*Exit Ophelia.*

Painted by BENJAMIN WEST, PRESIDENT R.A.

Engraved by FRANCIS LEGAT.

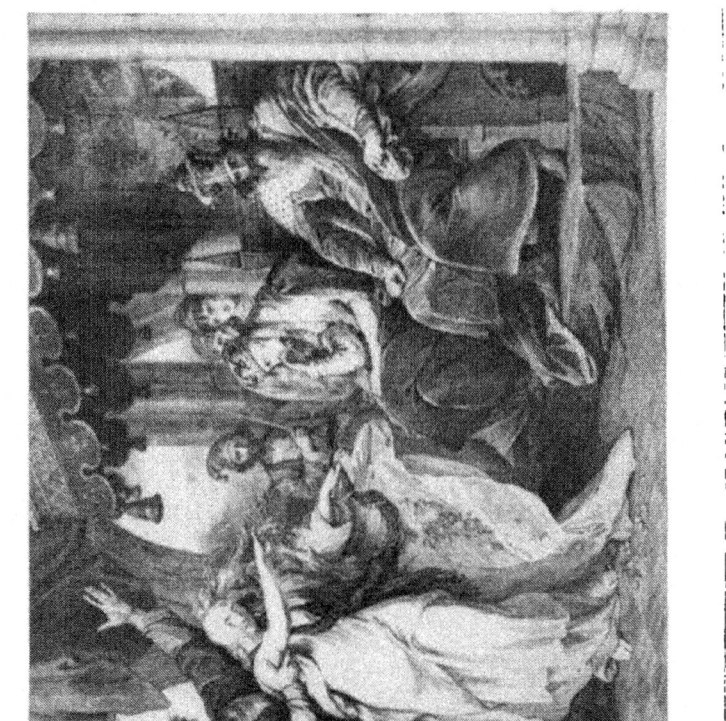

PH. LXXXIII.

KING LEAR.

(1)

LXXXIV.

KING LEAR.

Act I. Scene 1.

KING LEAR'S PALACE.

Lear, Cornwall, Albany, Goneril, Regan, Cordelia, King of France, Duke of Burgundy, Kent, Attendants, &c.

   Cor. Why have my sisters husbands, if they say
They love you, all? Haply, when I shall wed,
That lord whose hand must take my plight shall carry
Half my love with him, half my care, and duty:
Sure, I shall never marry like my sisters,
[To love my father all.]
   Lear. But goes thy heart with this?
   Cor.   Ay, my good lord.
   Lear. So young, and so untender?
   Cor. So young, my lord, and true.
   Lear. Let it be so:—Thy truth then be thy dower:
For, by the sacred radiance of the sun;
The mysteries of Hecate and the night;
By all the operation of the orbs,
From whom we do exist, and cease to be;
Here I disclaim all my paternal care,
Propinquity and property of blood,
And as a stranger to my heart and me
Hold thee, from this, for ever.—

        Painted by HENRY FUSELI, R.A.
        Engraved by RICHARD EARLOM.

Pl. LXXXIV.

KING LEAR.

(2)

LXXXV.

KING LEAR.

Act III. Scene 4.

PART OF A HEATH, WITH A HOVEL.

Lear, Kent, Fool, Edgar, disguised as a Madman, and Gloster, with a torch.

Lear. Thou wert better in a grave, than to answer with thy uncovered body this extremity of the skies.—Is man no more than this? Consider him well: Thou owest the worm no silk, the beast no hide, the sheep no wool, the cat no perfume:—Ha! here's three of us are sophisticated!—Thou art the thing itself: unaccommodated man is no more but such a poor, bare, forked animal as thou art.—Off, off, you lendings:—Come; unbutton here.—

[*Tearing off his clothes.*

Fool. Prithee, nuncle, be contented; 't is a naughty night to swim in.—Now a little fire in a wild field were like an old lecher's heart,—a small spark, all the rest of his body cold.—Look, here comes a walking fire.

Painted by BENJAMIN WEST, PRESIDENT R.A.
Engraved by WILLIAM SHARP.

Ph. LXXXV.

KING LEAR.

LXXXVI.

KING LEAR.

Act V. Scene 3.

A CAMP NEAR DOVER.

Lear, with Cordelia dead in his arms; Edgar, Albany, and Kent. Regan, Goneril, and Edmund, all dead.

 Edm. He hath commission from thy wife and me
To hang Cordelia in the prison, and
To lay the blame upon her own despair,
That she fordid herself.
 Alb. The gods defend her! Bear him hence awhile.
       [*Edmund is borne off.*

Enter Lear, with Cordelia dead in his arms; Edgar, Officer, and others.

 Lear. Howl, howl, howl!—O, you are men of stones;
Had I your tongues and eyes, I'd use them so
That heaven's vault should crack:—She's gone for ever!—
I know when one is dead, and when one lives;
She's dead as earth.—

  Painted by JAMES BARRY, R.A.
  Drawn and Engraved by FRANCIS LEGAT.

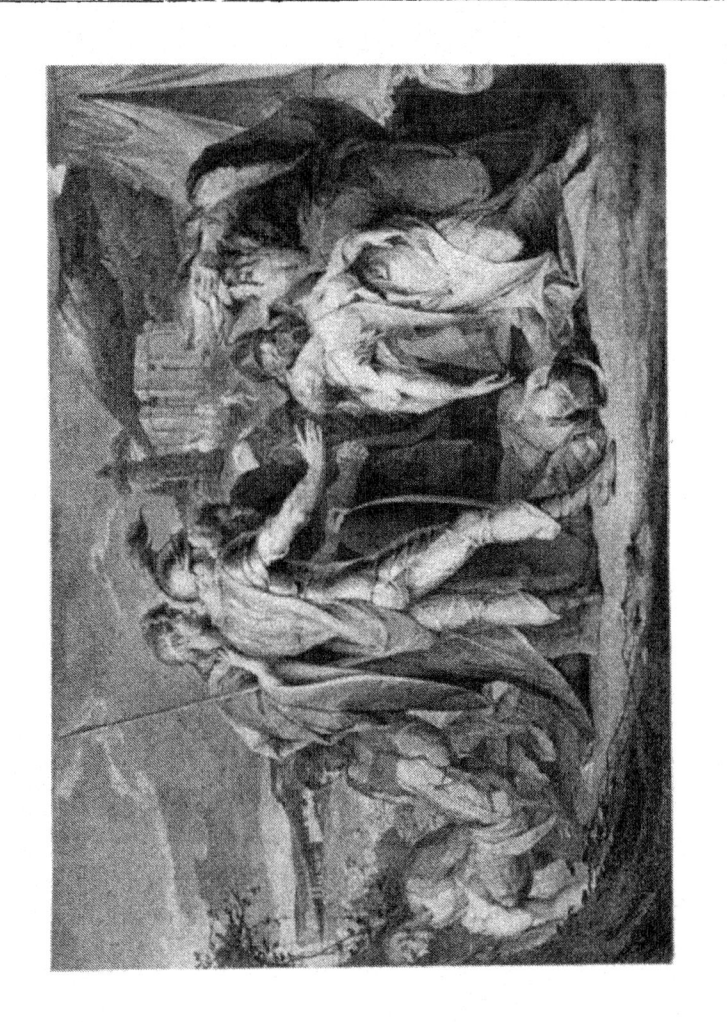

Ph. LXXXVI.

OTHELLO.

(1)

LXXXVII.

OTHELLO.

Act II. Scene 1.

CYPRUS; A PLATFORM NEAR THE SEA.

Desdemona, Othello, Iago, Cassio, Roderigo, Emilia, &c.

   Oth. O my fair warrior!
   Des.   My dear Othello!
   Oth. It gives me wonder great as my content,
To see you here before me. O my soul's joy!
If after every tempest come such calms,
May the winds blow till they have waken'd death!
And let the labouring bark climb hills of seas,
Olympus-high; and duck again as low
As hell's from heaven! If it were now to die,
'T were now to be most happy; for, I fear
My soul hath her content so absolute,
That not another comfort like to this
Succeeds in unknown fate.

Painted by THOMAS STOTHARD, R.A.
Engraved by THOMAS RYDER.

Pl. LXXXVII.

OTHELLO.

(2)

LXXXVIII.

OTHELLO.

Act V. Scene 2.

A BEDCHAMBER.

Othello, Desdemona in bed, asleep.

Oth. It is the cause, it is the cause, my soul,—
Let me not name it to you, you chaste stars!—
It is the cause.——Yet I 'll not shed her blood;
Nor scar that whiter skin of hers than snow,
And smooth as monumental alabaster.
                                          [Takes off his sword.
Yet she must die, else she 'll betray more men.
Put out the light, and then —— Put out the light?
If I quench thee, thou flaming minister!
I can again thy former light restore,
Should I repent me:—but once put out thy light,
Thou cunning'st pattern of excelling nature,
I know not where is that Promethean heat
That can thy light relume. When I have pluck'd thy rose,
I cannot give it vital growth again,
It needs must wither: I 'll smell thee on the tree.—
                                                 [Kissing her.
O balmy breath, that doth almost persuade
Justice to break her sword!—One more, one more.—
Be thus when thou art dead, and I will kill thee,
And love thee after: One more, and that 's the last:
So sweet was ne'er so fatal.—

Painted by JAMES GRAHAM.
Engraved by WILLIAM LENEY.

Рв. LXXXVIII.   351

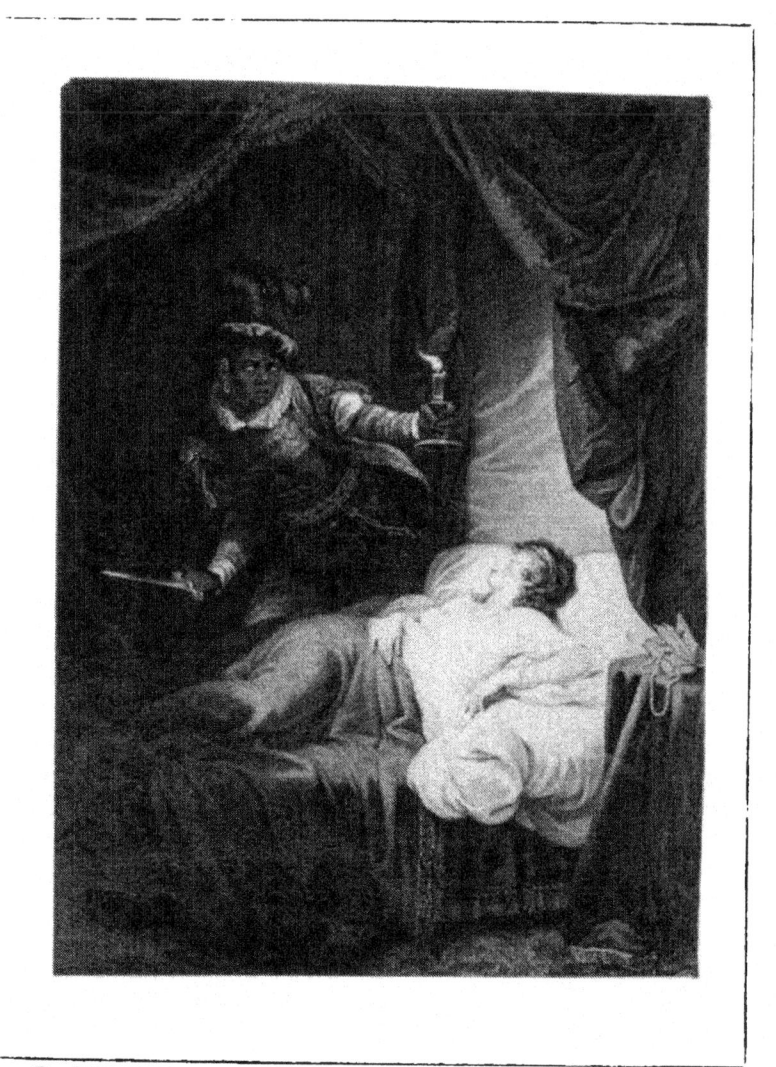

OTHELLO.

(3)

LXXXIX.

OTHELLO.

Act V. Scene 2.

A BEDCHAMBER.

Othello, Desdemona in bed, asleep.

   Oth. ——— I must weep,
But they are cruel tears: This sorrow 's heavenly;
It strikes where it doth love.—She wakes—
   Des. Who 's there? Othello?
   Oth. Ay, Desdemona.
   Des. Will you come to bed, my lord?
   Oth. Have you pray'd to-night, Desdemon?
   Des. Ay, my lord.

Painted by JOSIAH BOYDELL.
Engraved by WILLIAM LENEY.

Pit. LXXXIX

ANTONY AND CLEOPATRA.

(1)

XC.

ANTONY AND CLEOPATRA.

Act III. Scene 9.

ALEXANDRIA; THE PALACE.

Antony, Cleopatra, Eros, Charmian, Iras, &c.

Eros. The queen, my lord, the queen.
Iras. Go to him, madam, speak to him;
He is unqualitied with very shame.
Cleo. Well then,—Sustain me:—O!
Eros. Most noble sir, arise; the queen approaches;
Her head's declin'd, and death will seize her; but
Your comfort makes the rescue.
Ant. I have offended reputation;
A most unnoble swerving.
Eros.   Sir, the queen.
Ant. O, whither hast thou led me, Egypt? See,
How I convey my shame out of thine eyes
By looking back on what I have left behind
'Stroy'd in dishonour.

Painted by HENRY TRESHAM, R.A.
Engraved by GEORGE SIGMUND *and* JOHN GOTTLIEB FACIUS.

Pl. XC.

THE NEW YORK
PUBLIC LIBRARY

ASTOR, LENOX
TILDEN FOUNDATIONS

ANTONY AND CLEOPATRA.

(2)

XCI.

ANTONY AND CLEOPATRA.

Act V. Scene 2.

(BASSO-RELIEVO.)

ALEXANDRIA; A ROOM IN THE MONUMENT.

Cleopatra and Charmian; Iras dead.

Cleo. This proves me base
If she first meet the curled Antony,
He'll make demand of her; and spend that kiss
Which is my heaven to have. Come, thou mortal wretch,
    [*To the asp, which she applies to her breast.*
With thy sharp teeth this knot intrinsicate
Of life at once untie: poor venomous fool,
Be angry, and despatch. O, couldst thou speak!
That I might hear thee call great Cæsar, ass
Unpolicied!
    Char.   O eastern star!
    Cleo.   Peace, peace!
Dost thou not see my baby at my breast,
That sucks the nurse asleep?
    Char.   O, break! O, break!
    Cleo. As sweet as balm, as soft as air, as gentle,—
O Antony!—Nay, I will take thee too:—
    [*Applying another asp to her arm.*
What should I stay—

Modelled by The Hon. ANNE SEYMOUR DAMER.

Engraved by THOMAS HELLYER.

PH. XCI.

CYMBELINE.

(1)

XCII.

CYMBELINE.

Act I. Scene 2.

BRITAIN; THE GARDEN OF CYMBELINE'S PALACE.

Imogen, Posthumus, Queen, Cymbeline, &c.

   Post.   Should we be taking leave
As long a term as yet we have to live,
The loathness to depart would grow: Adieu!
   Imo. Nay, stay a little:
Were you but riding forth to air yourself,
Such parting were too petty. Look here, love;
This diamond was my mother's: take it, heart;
But keep it till you woo another wife,
When Imogen is dead.
   Post. How! how! another?—
You gentle gods, give me but this I have,
And sear up my embracements from a next
With bonds of death!—Remain, remain thou here
                            [*Putting on the ring.*
While sense can keep it on! And sweetest, fairest,
As I my poor self did exchange for you,
To your so infinite loss; so, in our trifles
I still win of you: For my sake wear this;
It is a manacle of love; I'll place it
Upon this fairest prisoner.
                  [*Putting a bracelet on her arm.*

Painted by WILLIAM HAMILTON, R.A.

Engraved by THOMAS BURKE.

Рис. XCII.

CYMBELINE.

(2)

XCIII.

CYMBELINE.

Act III. Scene 4.

NEAR MILFORD HAVEN.

Pisanio and Imogen.

 Imo. ———— Come, fellow, be thou honest:
Do thou thy master's bidding: When thou see'st him
A little witness my obedience: Look!
I draw the sword myself: take it; and hit
The innocent mansion of my love, my heart:
Fear not; 't is empty of all things but grief:
Thy master is not there; who was, indeed,
The riches of it: Do his bidding; strike.
Thou mayst be valiant in a better cause,
But now thou seem'st a coward.
 Pis.   Hence, vile instrument!
Thou shalt not damn my hand.
 Imo.   Why, I must die;
And if I do not by thy hand, thou art
No servant of thy master's: Against self-slaughter
There is a prohibition so divine
That cravens my weak hand. Come, here 's my heart;
Something 's afore 't;—Soft, soft; we 'll no defence;
Obedient as the scabbard.

Painted by JOHN HOPPNER, R.A.
Engraved by ROBERT THEW.

Рис. XCIII.

CYMBELINE.

XCIV.

CYMBELINE.

Act III. Scene 6.

BEFORE THE CAVE OF BELARIUS.

Imogen in Boy's Clothes.

Imo. —————— But what is this?
Here is a path to it: 'Tis some savage hold:
I were best not call; I dare not call: yet famine,
Ere clean it o'erthrow nature makes it valiant.
Plenty, and peace, breeds cowards; hardness ever
Of hardiness is mother.—Ho! who's here?
If any thing that's civil, speak;—if savage—
Take, or lend.—Ho!—No answer? then I'll enter.
Best draw my sword; and if mine enemy
But fear the sword like me, he'll scarcely look on 't.
Such a foe, good heavens!

Painted by RICHARD WESTALL, R.A.
Engraved by THOMAS GAUGAIN.

Ph. XCIV.

THE NEW YORK PUBLIC LIBRARY
REFERENCE DEPARTMENT

This book is under no circumstances to be taken from the Building

JAN 1 5 1916		
JAN 1 8 1916	MAR 1 0 1917	
JAN 2 6 1916		
JAN 2 7 1916		
JAN 2 8 1916		
MAR 1916		
APR 1 1916		
APR 2 7 1916		
JUN - 5 1916		

form 410

THE NEW YORK PUBLIC LIBRARY
REFERENCE DEPARTMENT

This book is under no circumstances to be taken from the Building

form 410